Be Nintendo Masters

---

*Clayton Walnum &
Andy Eddy*

To Lynn and Bissy

©1990 by Clayton Walnum and Andy Eddy

FIRST EDITION
FIRST PRINTING—1990

All rights reserved. No part of this book shall be reproduced, stored in a retrieval system, or transmitted by any means, electronic, mechanical, photocopying, recording, or otherwise, without written permission from the publisher. No patent liability is assumed with respect to the use of the information contained herein. While every precaution has been taken in the preparation of this book, the publisher and author assume no responsibility for errors or omissions. Neither is any liability assumed for damages resulting from the use of the information contained herein.

International Standard Book Number: 0-672-48483-8
Library of Congress Catalog Card Number: 90-61220

Acquisitions Editor: *Marie Butler-Knight*
Manuscript Editor: *Joe Kraynak*
Production Coordinator: *Becky Imel*
Designer: *Glenn Santner*
Illustrator: *Alan Hunter*
Cover Artist: *Ned Shaw*
Production: *Brad Chinn, Sally Copenhaver, Tami Hughes, William Hurley, Charles Hutchinson, Jodi Jensen, Lori Lyons, Jennifer Matthews, Joe Ramon, Dennis Sheehan, Mary Beth Wakefield*

Printed in the United States of America

Contents

Foreword, v

Introduction, viii

Fantasy, 3

Zelda II: The Adventure of Link, 3
Dragon Warrior, 10
Faxanadu, 16
Castlevania II: Simon's Quest, 24
Ultima: Exodus, 31
Shadowgate, 43

Science Fiction, 53

Bionic Commando, 53
Super C, 62

Military, 71

Strider, *71*
Metal Gear, *77*
Defender of the Crown, *82*

Arcade, 93

Super Mario Bros. 3, *93*
Mega Man 2, *100*
Teenage Mutant Ninja Turtles, *108*

Action & Sports, 117

Batman, *117*
Double Dragon II, *124*
World Championship Wrestling, *131*

Super Secrets!, 137

Secrets, *137*

Manufacturers, 147

Foreword

by Orson Scott Card

Getting Inside the Game

A good video game makes you feel as though you're in a strange new world, full of danger and excitement. At every turn, you face a new challenge. At every station, you encounter a new puzzle or a stronger opponent. Defeat the enemy, solve the new puzzle, and you get to explore deeper into the game world, to take on more difficult foes.

That's how a good video game makes you *feel*, but in fact it's all illusion. The game is just a bunch of dots on a screen and sounds coming out of a speaker. And you aren't really wiping out entire armies and swinging a saber—you're just mashing and twisting a plastic controller while you sit in your living room in Whatever Town, USA.

Behind those dots on the screen, there's a computer program that's telling the Nintendo machine which dots to put where, which sounds to push out of the speaker, and what to do when you fiddle around with the controller. Inside that program are all the deep dark secrets of how the game works. And, therefore, how to beat the thing.

That's where Clayton Walnum and Andy Eddy come in. They know computers so well that some of them call Clay and Andy their cousins. As for programmers and designers—well, they have other names for Clay and Andy. You see, with Clay and Andy around, none of their secrets are safe, and that makes them none too happy.

What kind of secrets? Why the solutions to the puzzles, of course. As often as not, the solution requires you to make some off-the-wall connection that no one in his right mind would ever think of. But Clayton Walnum is a natural, and sometimes it takes a slightly twisted mind to figure out how the game designer thinks.

The programmer, on the other hand, is as sane and level-headed as any person who lives entirely on beer, nachos, and gummy bears can possibly be. But the programmer is also fundamentally lazy. He takes the game design and figures out the most efficient program to make the right stuff happen on the screen at the right time.

And sometimes the "most efficient" program has a loophole somewhere, a back-door solution to the problem. This is especially helpful when you're in one of those killer situations where it looks like the game is going to kill you no matter what you do. To save yourself, you need to think like a programmer—figure out how the program works and find your way through that back door.

You need to think like a computer, figure out the patterns, *without* getting distracted. Once you realize that Bad Guy X always kicks after punching with his right hand—or always swoops way to the right when he starts out with that twisting pattern in the upper left corner of the screen—then you can anticipate his next move and waste him.

But that's not always easy to see when you're fighting twenty or thirty guys at once. That's why Clayton Walnum is such a decent person to have around. He's like the guy at the arcade who stops and watches you for a couple of seconds and, without getting obnoxious about it, says, "Why don't you try waiting over there for a couple of seconds and then come out and get him from behind?" Then he disappears and you're on your own again—armed with just enough know-how to get on.

What Clay and Andy can't do is supply you with quick reflexes and instantaneous judgment. If you didn't get those from your parents' zygotes, you're out of luck. But that's the way you want it. Even after you've memorized every hint and clue and trick that Walnum and Eddy tell you in this book, you're still the one who has to get into the game world and *do* it. You're the one who has to make the judgment calls at just the right time. You're the one who has to make that controller stand up and dance. And when you win, *you're* the master of the game!

Orson Scott Card, computer game critic for *Compute!*, is the only science fiction author to win both the Nebula and Hugo awards two years running. He is also the winner of the World Fantasy Award and the John W. Campbell Memorial Award. A prolific writer, his science fiction and fantasy novels include *Speaker for the Dead, Seventh Son, Red Prophet, Songmaster, Treason,* and *Ender's Game,* the ultimate computer-game novel.

Introduction

This book is worth $382.50.

Don't believe it? Then consider this: Only a few video games are ever played to the end, with most players giving up about halfway through. Based on an average price of $45, each unfinished game then represents $22.50 lost. Seventeen game strategies are included in this book, each of which will help make you a winner. Seventeen times $22.50 is $382.50. You see?

Not convinced? Then consider also that the games represented here were carefully chosen due to their popularity and difficulty. Chances are you own these games. Chances are you haven't finished them.

But let's get specific. Unlike many so-called strategy guides, the chapters that comprise this book are not reworkings of game manuals. They are in-depth strategies, each of which covers a particular game from beginning to end. This isn't a buyer's guide. Nor is it a collection of reviews. This book is help. Real help.

Of course, in order to get help from this book, you must know how to use it. Following are four important guidelines.

Before this book can help you, you must be skilled in the basics of arcade gameplay. This is a book for advanced players. If you've never touched a control pad before, put this book back on your shelf. Now sit down with a game like *Super Mario Bros. 3* and learn how to control your on-screen character. No book can teach you that skill.

Play the game before consulting the book. I can't stress this enough. Never read the strategy for a game until you really need help. This goes double for adventure games, since solving puzzles is a major part of their challenge. Nothing ruins a game more than reading about secrets that would have been more fun to discover on your own. If you don't own one of the games included in this book and would like to learn more about it, read the game summary at the beginning of the chapter. Do not, however, read past the "General Strategy" section unless you need help.

Read the "General Strategy" and "Strategies" sections first. Each chapter starts with an overview of the game and general hints on gameplay. The further you get into the chapter, the more detailed the hints become. Avoid the temptation to read more than you need to.

When you win a game, read its chapter from beginning to end. Even though you've won a particular game, you never know what awesome stuff you might have missed. These are complex games, crammed with fun surprises. Why miss out on anything?

Now that you know how to get the most from this book, here's a special surprise. At the end of the book, you'll find our Super Secrets, a list of fun things to try for over 50 additional games. Some Super Secrets provide important help. Others are just amusing. Whatever the case, try as many as you can. They're a blast.

Hey! Wait a minute. With all those Super Secrets, maybe this book is worth more than $382.50. Let's see. If the average video game is 50 hours long, and one Super Secret adds an extra 20 minutes of fun, then 50 times 20 is . . .

Aw, never mind. Go play some games.

And win.

Clayton Walnum
April, 1990

Acknowledgments

For expert gaming advice and other services above and beyond the call of duty, we wish to acknowledge Gregory Gruber, Alan Hunter, Barry Kolbe, Philip Kolbe, Donn Nauert, Peter Smith, and Michio Tsuzuki. For the superb illustrations at the beginning of each section, we thank Alan Hunter. We would also like to express appreciation to our acquisitions editor, Marie Butler-Knight, for her support and enthusiasm over the course of this project, and to our manuscript editor, Joe Kraynak, for fixing all the little things. Finally, we are particularly grateful to our families for living without us for the hundreds of hours it took to create this book.

Alan Hunter is an award-winning illustrator who has designed graphics for over 150 movie posters, advertisements, and video-cassette boxes. He has also had the honor of being chosen to design the Cannes Film Festival invitation. Over 40 of Alan's illustrations have appeared on the covers and pages of various publications, including *Life, Time, VideoGames & Computer Entertainment, PC LapTop Computers,* and *Billboard*.

Clayton Walnum, contributing editor for *VideoGames & Computer Entertainment*, has been writing about computers and video games for nearly 10 years. A former magazine editor, his articles have appeared in such publications as *The Writer, ANALOG Computing, VideoGames & Computer Entertainment, ST-Log,* and *Atari Explorer*. He lives in Connecticut with his wife, Lynn, and his three children, Christopher, Justin, and Stephen.

Andy Eddy is the Executive Editor of *VideoGames & Computer Entertainment* and an avid gamer, twice having held the world record for Atari's *Battlezone* arcade game. During his six years of writing about electronic games and computers, he has appeared on television and has been published or quoted in magazines including *VideoGames & Computer Entertainment, TV Guide, Boy's Life, Compute!,* and *ANALOG Computing*. Andy lives in California with his wife, Bissy, and his two children, Brian and Meghan.

Trademark Acknowledgments

All terms mentioned in this book that are known to be trademarks or service marks are listed below. In addition, terms suspected of being trademarks or service marks have been appropriately capitalized. Howard W. Sams & Company cannot attest to the accuracy of this information. Use of a term in this book should not be regarded as affecting the validity of any trademark or service mark.

Nintendo®, Nintendo Entertainment System®, Faxanadu™, Dragon Warrior™, Zelda II: The Adventure of Link™, and Super Mario Bros. 3™ are trademarks of Nintendo of America Inc.

Strider™, Bionic Commando™, Mega Man 2™, and CAPCOM™ are trademarks of CAPCOM U.S.A. Inc.

Defender of the Crown™ is a trademark of Cinemaware Corp.

Ultima® is a trademark of Richard Garriott.

Metal Gear™ and Konami® are trademarks of Konami Industries Co. Ltd.

Shadowgate™ is a trademark of ICOM Simulations, Inc.

Simon's Quest™ and Super C™ are trademarks of Konami Inc.

Double Dragon II: The Revenge™ is a trademark of Technos Japan.

Acclaim™ is a trademark of Acclaim Entertainment, Inc.

Ultra® is a trademark of Ultra Software Corporation.

Sunsoft® is a trademark of Sun Corporation of America.

Batman™ is a trademark of DC Comics Inc.

Teenage Mutant Ninja Turtles®, Leonardo™, Raphael™, Michaelangelo™, Donatello™, April™, Shredder™, Splinter™, Technodrome™, Party Wagon™, Mouser™, Big Mouser™, Foot Soldier™, Bebop™, and Rocksteady™ are trademarks of Mirage Studios, U.S.A.

FANTASY

Fantasy

Zelda II: The Adventure of Link

Company: *Nintendo*
Type: *Arcade/Adventure*

The Game

Objective: To locate the hints, equipment, and spells necessary to make it through the seven palaces and defeat Ganon.

Organization: The land of Hyrule—including swamps, mountains, forests, and plains—is displayed as a large, scrolling, map through which you must guide Link to towns, caves, palaces, and other locations. When Link enters a location, the game display changes from overhead view to side view, where most of the action takes place.

Creatures: Hyrule is crawling with every type of meany you can imagine, including bit-bots, stalfos, rat warriors, iron-knuckles, and gargoyles. The bosses, one in each palace, include Horsehead, Gooma, Barba, Carock, Helmethead, and Ironknuckle.

General Strategy: Continually increase your strength; avoid battles only when absolutely necessary. If a location is too difficult to complete, you probably don't have an item you need or haven't yet built up enough strength. Learn to use magic effectively; if you don't, you'll never finish the game. Search everywhere. Some important items are shrewdly hidden.

The Controls

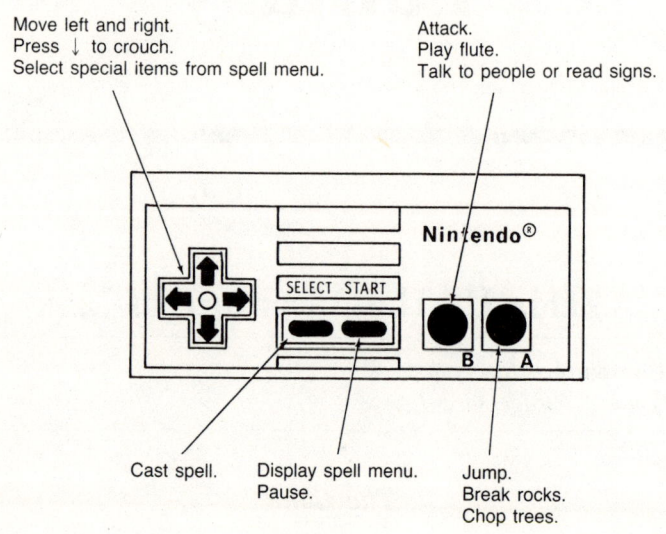

The Challenge

This is a huge game. Few players will manage to make it through all the challenges and defeat Ganon. Nevertheless, it's your duty as Link (and as a Nintendo Master Gamer) to keep a stiff upper lip. Fight, fight, fight. And when all else fails, feed the game cartridge to your dog.

Strategies

The creatures in *Zelda II* display little imagination. They'll attack, over and over, in exactly the same pattern. Learn their weaknesses. Then clobber them.

Remember, fighting is important. It makes you strong. It makes you skilled. And, yes, sometimes it makes you dead. By fighting, you earn experience points that you can use to buy additional levels of attack, life, or magic. If you don't build your character by getting into a some scuffles, you won't advance.

Explore every inch of Hyrule. Many useful items—one-ups, treasure bags, magic jars, hearts, fairies—are hidden throughout the countryside. Some items are a must.

Also, when you're in a palace, whack your sword against every statue you find. Many contain magic jars. Some contain angry monsters. Be prepared to fight.

Frequently, when you defeat an enemy, a magic jar appears. An inexperienced player will grab the jar without thinking. Resist the temptation. Check your magic meter first to make sure it has room for more of that good ol' spell juice. If it doesn't, it's a waste to grab the jar right away.

In the case of a full magic meter, first cast a spell. (The magic shield is always useful.) That'll bring the meter down. Since the magic jar will restore your magic anyway, the spell you cast is free.

This technique is especially important for the red magic jars, since they restore your magic meter completely, no matter how low it is. When you get a red jar, cast every spell you can. You'll hate yourself if you don't take advantage of a free spell and then later discover that you needed it. Wasting magic makes you grumpy.

In addition to healers and informants, most towns have a wise man who can teach you a handy spell. However, in most cases, the wise man only greets you if you've performed some service for the town, such as finding a missing trophy or rescuing a kidnapped child. Many times, you can meet the objectives of these mini-quests in caves.

When you enter a town, talk to everybody. Keep talking until you're positive there's nothing new to learn. Much of what you discover will guide you toward puzzle solutions. Write down all that the townspeople say. You may think you'll remember every clue. You won't.

Before Parapa Palace

Your first destination is Parapa Palace. But before you go there, build up your strength. Start by getting the magic shield spell in Rauru—you won't get hurt half as bad in battle.

Somewhere near Tantari Desert, north of North Castle, is a treasure bag worth 50 experience points. Get that bag to immediately increase your level.

Roam the forests of Hyrule, fighting creatures. When your life meter gets low, boogie on over to Rauru or Ruto, and get healed for free.

Enter no caves. Without the candle, caves are dark and dangerous.

Parapa Palace

Parapa Palace is way up in the northeast corner of the Hyrule mainland. Get there via the cave east of Rauru. I know, I told you not to enter caves without the candle. But this cave is an exception—it's short and you'll only have to deal with one creature.

After the cave, don't go straight to the palace. Tucked away in the desert, you'll find a heart, which will extend your life meter.

Once you have the heart, go to the palace. Your goal is to find all of the keys and obtain the candle. (You'll need the keys to unlock the golden gates in the corridors.) In Parapa Palace, you'll run into rat warriors, bouncing faces, stalfos, ironknuckles, and the ubiquitous bit bots.

Parapa Palace's boss is a creature called Horsehead. After defeating him, place a crystal in the stone statue and vamoose. If you have a tough time with Horsehead, here's a hint—stay to the far left of the screen.

The Caves

Once you have the candle, you can see when you're inside caves. Search the cave south of North Castle. You'll find something helpful there. The cave in Tantari Desert contains an item that'll please the residents of Ruto.

I won't say much more about caves. Just remember that each one either contains an important item or leads to a new location. Overlook none.

Midoro Palace

Midoro Palace is hidden deep in a swamp on the other side of the mountains south of North Castle. Before going to Midoro

Palace, visit Saria, where you'll find an important spell. Fight more enemies and build experience points.

In Parapa Palace, you'll meet a couple of new creatures—the flying and walking gargoyles. (Makes my neck prickle just thinking about them.) As usual, find all keys, then defeat the boss. Also, locate the glove.

The boss is a baddy named Helmethead. This guy's tough. You have to knock off two helmets in order to expose his ugly face. Only then can you start doing some damage.

Death Mountain Maze

To get to Death Mountain, persuade the gatekeeper in Saria to give you bridge privileges. You'll need a note from Bagu. As luck would have it, Bagu isn't home, so you'll have to find him.

Once over the bridge, find the best path through the maze. It's a tough job, but somebody's got to do it. Why? To get the hammer, of course.

Island Palace

With the hammer, you can break the rock that blocks the path to Mido, where you'll find two important items. Don't leave Mido until you've located them both.

Got 'em? Great! Now it's off to Island Palace. Trouble is, you have to be a good swimmer to get there. Or do you? Could there be a secret tunnel? (Nudge nudge, wink wink.) Do some exploring. Hint: A king is doing the long sleep—and I mean the *long* sleep—somewhere near the tunnel.

Island Palace is a neat place (if you don't mind dying)—it contains many interesting rooms and scads of new monsters. You'll fight mace throwers, flying eyes, and shooting gargoyles, just to name a few. Make sure your sword is sharp.

In Island Palace, find the raft, which will take you across the ocean to East Hyrule. Also, find a slew of keys.

At the end of Island Palace, you'll face Ironknuckle, the boss. He attacks by horse, so you must first dismount him. The downward stab technique is invaluable here.

Got the raft? Head for the dock!

Maze Island Palace

Next stop—Maze Island. Here you'll visit two towns. Nabooru is easy to get to and is a great place to have your life and magic restored. Get a new spell too.

The second town, Darunia, is in a desert northwest of Nabooru. Two valuable items await you. If you have a hard time getting someone to open a door, think like Santa Claus.

Maze Island Palace is your toughest challenge yet. Some new enemies, the wizards, are particularly frustrating. They appear and disappear, all the while casting waves of magical energy. Your reflect spell is effective here.

In addition to powerful monsters, Maze Island Palace has some treacherous traps, such as bottomless rooms. Look out below!

Items of interest are the winged boots, which will let you walk on water, and Carock, the boss. Carock is a powerful wizard, but he's particularly susceptible to your reflect spell.

By the way, explore the entire maze, not just the route to the palace. You'll be glad you did.

The Fifth Palace

It's time to try out those winged boots. South of the maze is another island, on which rests the Fifth Palace. To get there, walk on water. Hint—there's more than one path in the ocean. The Fifth Palace isn't the only place you can go with your winged boots.

By now, you should have a strong character. Fighting to gain experience points is less important now. Your goal is to stay alive. In other words, avoid battles.

If your life energy gets low, a couple of rooms in this palace contain unlimited monsters. They keep on coming no matter how many you kill, proving that the average monster has the brain of a toaster. Gather those magic jars.

Points of interest in the Fifth Palace are fake walls (you can walk through them), the flute, fire witches, and Gooma, the boss. Gooma is easy to beat once you get the hang of it. Watch closely, and learn the timing of his swings.

New Kasuto

Been to Old Kasuto, the abandoned place with all the invisible monsters? Seems the residents got fed up with the rough neighborhood and built a new town. Of course, building a new town is a good defense only if the bad guys can't find it, right? Need some help? The village of New Kasuto is located in a small forest northeast of Three Eye Rock. Chop down trees.

If you expect certain people in New Kasuto to cooperate, you need the seven magic containers. If your magic meter isn't seven segments long, you don't have the complete set. Explore the ocean. Break every rock and check every cave.

By the way, not all New Kasuto's buildings are visible. Cast the right spell in the right place, and you'll get a surprise.

The Sixth Palace

What Sixth Palace? You mean you can't see it? That's probably because it's invisible. If you've listened to the townspeople's clues, you should know where it is. I will, however, give the confused an extra hint—when all is revealed, Three Eye Rock is more a diamond than a triangle, and the rocks love music.

The Sixth Palace is unusual in that you need the magic key to open the gates. Missing that wonderful item? Take another trip to New Kasuto.

In the Sixth Palace, locate the magic cross, which reveals invisible creatures. Also, defeat the boss, an ornery fire-breathing dragon called Barba. Hit him in the face as he rises. If you expect to live long enough to get the job done, you'd better be a good jumper.

The Grand Palace

Here you are at last, facing the final leg of your long and arduous journey. Don't order the pizza yet. The Grand Palace is the greatest challenge of all. Only the best will emerge victorious.

Just getting to the Grand Palace is tough enough to make Rambo cry. (The palace is in the mountains northwest of Old Kasuto.) Many dangerous caverns block your route, and wandering monsters attack frequently. The spell magic will serve you well. Use it.

Still, no matter how heroically you battle, by the time you reach the palace, you'll be two heartbeats from being issued a halo. Don't despair. Once at the Grand Palace's entrance, you'll continue from there each time you use up all your lives.

Since the rooms fit together illogically, mapping the Grand Palace is an exercise in frustration. Hang in there.

Your objective is to locate the Final Guardian and defeat him, after which you'll face Ganon himself. To defeat the Final Guardian, you must have the thunder spell. Moreover, your life and magic meters need to be full.

How can you fight through the palace and still have all your lives? Look for trick walls that hide secret rooms. One-ups and fairies will help you along. Warning—don't miss the secret tunnel, hidden under a block. Break every block you find.

Good luck!

Dragon Warrior

Company: *Nintendo*
Type: *Role-Playing Adventure*

The Game

Objective: To find and rescue Princess Gwaelin and destroy the Dragonlord.

Organization: The game is set in Alefgard, represented on your screen as a huge, scrolling map. Along with mountains, forests, swamps, and oceans, the map contains towns, castles, and caves. Caves usually contain mazes, while the towns have shops where you can buy supplies.

Creatures: At first, you'll battle weaker creatures, including slimes and drakees. Soon you'll be strong enough to handle ghosts, magicians, and scorpions. By the end of the game, you'll be matching brains and brawn with strong and intelligent creatures like dragons, starwyverns, and shadow knights.

General Strategy: Spend a lot of time searching out and destroying monsters. This is the only way to increase your experience points. It's also a good way to accumulate gold to buy supplies and better weapons. When visiting a village, talk to everyone. The hints the townspeople provide are essential.

The Controls

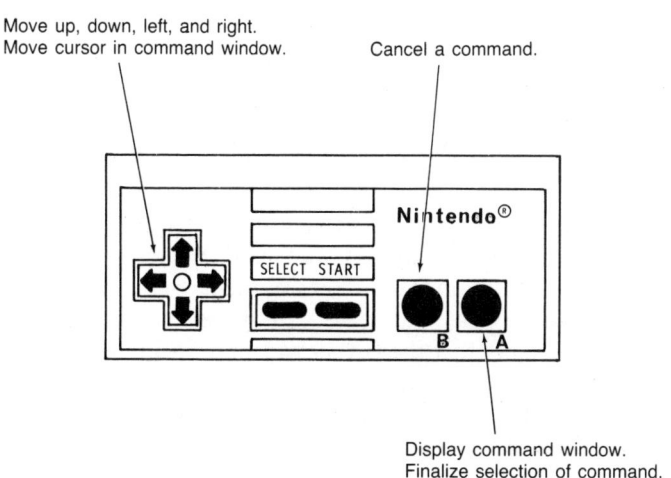

Move up, down, left, and right.
Move cursor in command window.

Cancel a command.

Display command window.
Finalize selection of command.

The Challenge

Okay, I admit it. I prefer turn-oriented games to real-time, action games. Maybe I'm getting old. Or maybe those blisters on my control-pad hand have been aching more than usual lately. Whatever the reason, *Dragon Warrior* is as fresh as a springtime breeze to this Nintendo Master Gamer. It's not that I don't like arcade games. I do. Really. It's just that games like *Dragon Warrior* are so rare that when one comes along I jump on it quicker than a flee jumps on a mutt.

Dragon Warrior gives you time to use that gray stuff between your ears, lets you plan your moves, consider your best strategy. You don't have to outmaneuver real-time creatures whose only reason for existence is to torment you until you're dribbling on your shirt and throwing valuable objects around the room. This is a thinking game, gentle on the nerves.

Don't get scared away. *Dragon Warrior* doesn't require any profound thinking. This isn't chess. Anyway, I've already put this puppy to bed. It's snoozing in my solved drawer, so I'm fully prepared to guide you on your journey through Alefgard.

Strategies

When playing *Dragon Warrior*, two strategies are most important—increase experience and gather clues. Concentrate on these two activities, and you'll rarely, if ever, come to any dead ends.

Spend most of your playing time getting experience points. More specifically, venture into the countryside of Alefgard and battle monsters. Lots of them. Until your experience is high enough, you'll have little success advancing in the game. Remember that the farther you go from Tantegel Castle, the tougher your foes. When the monsters in a region are too tough for you, retreat to an easier area and increase your experience. Even the head honcho, the Dragonlord himself, is easy to beat when you have a strong character. Hint—level 30 is the highest experience level.

Talk to every person in every city. Moreover, write down what they say. At first, some clues won't make much sense. But you'll want to refer to them later, when you discover new items and secrets. Write down not only the clue but also who said it and where. And while you're at it, record where you find important items. By keeping a complete record of your game play, you won't have to backtrack later.

Once you've gained some experience and gathered a good list of clues, look over your notes and think. This will help you take the next step of your quest.

Searching

At first, you might be tempted to spend a lot of time searching. For example, when a villager told me "Thou shalt find the Stones of Sunlight in Tantegel Castle," I immediately examined every inch of the castle, square by square, using the search command. This process took an hour, and I found nothing.

Don't make the same mistake. All items can be more easily found by studying clues, and thus determining exactly where an item is. Sometimes, you need to combine clues. When I learned from a townsperson that Tantegel Castle had a cellar, I combined that knowledge with the previous clue about the Stones of Sunlight. I knew I needed to find some cellar stairs and that the stones had to be in that cellar.

Fighting

Before completing *Dragon Warrior*, you'll dull your sword on the hides of more creatures than ten Marios could shake sticks at. Fighting is the only way to increase experience, and increase it you must. The trouble with fighting is that someone can get hurt—that is, you can die.

Whenever you die, you'll return with half your cash missing. Since money is almost as important as experience, it doesn't pay (yes, folks, that's a pun) to let the monsters win. Here's a couple of hints that'll make fighting less dangerous and more profitable.

First, whenever possible, fight near town, where a quick visit to an inn will restore your strength. Second, always, *always*, completely restore your hit points immediately after a battle—even if you think you have enough points for another fight. You can never be sure how tough the next opponent will be. Use your heal spell often. If you don't have the heal spell yet, carry herbs with you. When your magic or herbs get low, return to town.

Warning: Don't rely on the heal spell to save you in the midst of battle. Yes, you can restore hit points even in the fight mode. But you can't use the heal spell and attack your opponent at the same time. Since the spell may give you fewer hit points than your enemy's next attack will take away, you'll end up depleting your magic to no good end. (This is true only of the heal spell. The healmore spell, however, increases your hit points more than any single attack can take away.)

The Dungeons

In most caves and in some castles, you must explore a dungeon maze. Unfortunately, you can see only a small portion of the maze at a time. And, without some form of light, you can see nothing at all. You must have at least a torch, or better yet, the Radiant spell, which sheds more light. The larger the visible area, the less you must actually explore. If you see that a corridor is empty, why examine it further? (As far as I remember, nothing in the mazes is invisible or requires a search.)

Finally, map out the dungeon mazes! Mapping is the only way to verify that you've looked everywhere. Also, some mazes are more intricate than others, having multiple levels with many stairways. If you don't map well, noting which stairway goes where, you might never make it out.

Weapons, Armor, and Shields

At the beginning of the game, you can afford little more than clothes and a club, fine for some quick slime squashing and drakee smashing, but useless against most other creatures. Upgrade your weapon, armor, and shield as soon as possible. Some monsters can inflict more than 50 points of damage against a poorly outfitted warrior. Quality armor can decrease that damage to as little as one point.

The same is true of your weapon. The better the weapon, the more damage it'll do. Save your gold and buy the best weapon you can.

The Monsters

For the most part, the monsters in Alefgard exhibit fairly predictable fighting habits. Slimes, drakees, and ghosts are dumb creatures, so they attack blindly, never using magic. Creatures like the starwyverns and the wizards, however, are extremely intelligent, battle fiercely, and enjoy well-developed magical skills. As you move deeper and deeper into the game, it becomes important to learn your enemies' strategies.

Take the starwyvern, for example. This beast is difficult to defeat, thanks to its annoying habit of healing itself every time you lop off a few feathers. When facing one of these feathered freaks, start your attack with stopspell. Then, not only will the starwyvern be unable to heal itself, it'll also waste a turn when it tries, giving you an advantage.

Wizards present an altogether different problem. They attack with swords and the hurtmore spell. Hurtmore can inflict large amounts of damage, so stopspell isn't a bad idea here, either.

Before you destroy the Dragonlord, you're going to fight a castle-load of other creatures. So study their attack habits. Be prepared for battle, and don't get caught with your armor down.

A Basic Quest Outline

The following paragraphs give a brief overview of what you must do to beat *Dragon Warrior*.

When you begin a new character, stay close to Tantegel Castle and Brecconary (the city next to the castle). Your only objective at this point is to increase your character's experience until he can safely travel.

Once you've advanced three or four levels, explore the cave northwest of the castle. A message awaits you. After exploring that dungeon (and building up your experience), travel northwest to Garinham, a city with a mysterious graveyard.

Then it's off to eastern Alefgard and the city of Kol. Kol contains a mystery too, as well as more shops to explore and more townspeople to question. Rack up experience points in the countryside around Kol. You'll be heading south next, where the creatures are really nasty.

The area south of Garinham, but north of the legendary city of Hauksness, is a good place to build experience points. Except for a cave, though, there's little else of interest. South of Kol is another city, Rimuldor, where you can purchase some special magical items—items that by this time you'll be anxious to find.

At this point, if you're not up to around level 18, you'd better do a heap of fighting. It's time to travel to the last populated city, Cantlin, deep in the south of Alefgard. Vicious monsters cruise outside this city, which makes it an excellent place to build your character to his highest level. Cantlin's inn will keep you healthy.

On the home stretch, take your quest all the way south of Rimuldor, and then to Charlock, the Dragonlord's castle, where your wit and might will face the final test. May you return a hero!

Faxanadu

Company: *Nintendo*
Type: *Arcade Adventure*

The Game

Objective: To get the three Elven wells flowing; then locate and destroy the Evil One.

Organization: The game is set in the areas in and around the World Tree—all locations are shown in horizontal, scrolling scenes. Most scenes contain heavy arcade action, but others, especially the towns, are more passive, allowing you to concentrate on exploring and on gathering clues.

Creatures: Although they have no names, many unusual enemies inhabit the World Tree. In addition to the common enemies, you'll encounter and do battle with several boss creatures, including the giant bat monsters and ghost worms.

General Strategy: Like many adventure-type arcade games, it's important to build strength in order to advance to higher levels. Gather enough money so you can buy items in the shops. Before you start out on a long expedition in new territory, fill the empty slots in your inventory with red magic potion—this stuff heals you. Talk to the townspeople; they have important information.

The Controls

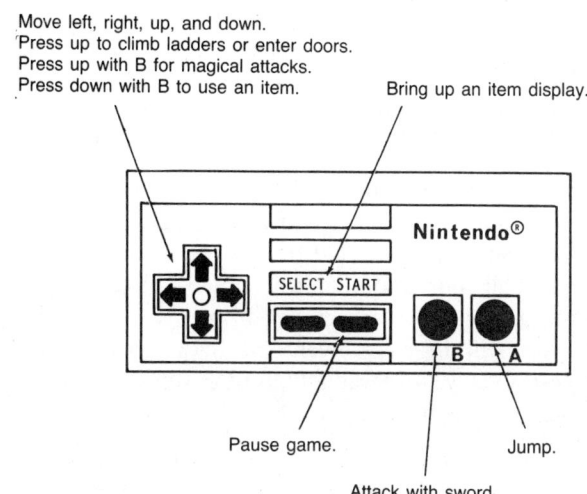

The Challenge

In the graphics department, *Faxanadu* is a rare treat. Some locations, especially near the end of the game, are downright spectacular. Combine excellent graphics with good game play (as *Faxanadu* does), and you get an almost unbeatable combination.

Strategies

As you travel from town to town, visit every shop and write down the items each sells. Some items cost more than you have, so you'll have to return later when you've packed more gold into your money bag. Wouldn't it be nice to know exactly where to shop for the item you need?

Don't cram your limited inventory with items you don't need right away. Save space for a good supply of red potions. Red potion is like blood. Without it you're doomed.

In order to build experience and accumulate cash, you must fight. Unfortunately, fighting is dangerous and may result in death. Death in turn results in the loss of the very cash and experience you were attempting to earn. The solution? Stay close to town. You'll fight better knowing the healer is close at hand.

Pay careful attention to your experience points. The instant you've earned enough experience for the next title, see the guru. Once you get a title, no one can take it away. But if you die before getting the title, the experience is lost.

Interested in unlimited cash? As you know, when you continue a game, you begin with a specific amount of gold. How much depends on your title. To get unlimited cash, try this—spend all your gold; then leave town and get killed. Continue the game. Your cash is replenished, yet the items you bought are still in your inventory. Great trick, huh? This works best if you've achieved a high title, since you then begin with a larger amount of money.

Some locations in *Faxanadu* are complicated, containing many interconnected rooms. Creating a map for these areas is essential. Draw a small square for each room—inside the square, note some landmark that will help you identify the room later. Most importantly, mark all exits, so you'll be sure to try every one. When marking exits, examine each room carefully. Some exits are hidden.

Use the following overall strategy to play this game. First, earn money and increase experience. During this phase of play, explore new areas, but stay close to town so you'll have easy access to the healer. Once you're strong enough for the next quest, explore farther from the city. Finally, when your explorations are complete, buy whatever items you need to access the next location. Then move on.

Because Faxandu cannot be easily broken down into levels, I'll organize the following discussion in terms of quests. Each quest represents a task that you must complete before moving on.

Quest 1

Enter the town of Eolis (you have no choice; the game starts here) and explore. You'll get some helpful clues, as well as some items you'll need to continue. The king will finance the beginning of your quest, but only if you have a certain ring.

Talk to everyone. They'll help you find what you need. During this portion of your quest, stay away from enemy creatures. You have no weapon—if something attacks, you're a goner.

With money from the king, visit Eolis's shops. Pick up a few essentials—a weapon, a key, and several red potions. Don't advance to the next quest until you've obtained these items.

Quest 2

After stocking up in Eolis, exit the town via the doorway on the far right. You'll need a key to unlock the door. You bought one, right?

The creatures in the area immediately beyond the door are wimps. Assuming you have a good supply of red potion, you should be able to make your way to the town of Apalune without mishap.

Quest 3

In the town of Apalune, and the areas beyond, the game really begins. After you arrive, enter every building and talk to all townspeople. Note what the shops have for sale. And don't overlook the shop just west of the town; it has some high-powered magic. Of course, powerful magic costs big dollarinos. (That's how hip people say "money." Cool, huh?) You may have to come back to this shop later—much later.

Your goal in quest 3 is to locate the mattock, a tool that can break the stones blocking the eastward path. First, investigate the area east of Apalune. This region is only four screens long—it's so small that if you can't get back to town alive, you should consider trading your Nintendo for a paint-by-numbers set.

When you enter the castle east of Apalune, you'll get a good taste of the challenges to come. Many new creatures inhabit its creepy hallways. Learn how they fight. You'll see them again.

In the castle's last room, the bat monster is hanging out. Relax. If you stay on the left-hand ledge, his fire can't reach you. Use magic to blast him from a distance. If you have no magic, swing your knife or sword. Kill this guy and the mattock is yours.

Quest 4

Use the mattock to chop through the blocks, and continue on to the town of Forepaw. When you arrive, ask for clues. Then build up your strength. Arm yourself with new weapons and stronger armor and magic.

Next, restore the three Elven fountains. Before you set off, fill your inventory with red potion. Then explore the area east of Forepaw, where you'll find two of the fountains. The first fountain is accessible only with winged boots. The third fountain lies behind a door that requires a special key.

Once you have the first fountain working, look for another locked door (climb up and to the left). This door is the entrance to a huge castle. The castle is so big, in fact, that you'll need to map as you explore. Do three things—get the elixir, find the old man who guards the second fountain, and get the joker key from the guru.

Ready for that last fountain? Okay! You should now have the key to the door at the bottom of the cliffs (near where you found the first fountain). Beyond the door, you'll find another bat monster. This one's tougher than the first one. Be quick, and you can run right past him. In the next room, you'll discover the third fountain and the ruby ring.

Quest 5

Remember the fountain room with the two doors? If you recall, the left-hand door was enclosed by stone blocks. Well, it still is, and, in order to begin quest 5, you must enter that door. Don't despair. With the ruby ring you just won, you can shove away the stone on the top of the fountain. So what, you say? What do you care about a stupid stone on top of a stupid fountain? Well, when the stupid stone is moved, a stupid ladder to the stupid door appears. Not so stupid, after all. That door (you know, the stupid one) leads into the World of Mist, a creepy and mysterious place shrouded in fog.

Upon entering the World of Mist, travel to Mascon—go left, up, and right. As usual, build your experience while near the safety of the town. Upgrade your weapons.

There's little of value west of Mascon. Explore if you like. One castle, far to the northwest, provides battle practice against some new creatures. Your destiny, however, lies to the east.

It's difficult to see clearly in the World of Mist. For that reason, be alert when mapping. Overlook no exits. Some exits, high above you, can be reached only by clever jumping or by using the winged boots. Wherever there's a place not blocked by a stone, there's an exit.

Your objective for quest 5 is the pendant, a necklace that increases the power of your sword. Travel east from Mascon to find the castle where this prize is hidden. You'll find several other castles along the way. Some house concerned citizens, ready with clues; others hide dwarfs and other enemies ready to attack.

The castle containing the pendant is a complex labyrinth, but it's not overly large. Search for the bat monsters. Defeat two of these savage creatures, and the pendant appears.

Quest 6

Quest 6 is set in yet another region of the World of Mist. To get to this area, look for a ladder—you need the winged boots to reach it.

Your first destination is the town of Victim, which lies east of your entry point. I'll not tell you to gather clues, increase your experience, and upgrade your weapons. (Whoops. I think I just did.)

To the east of Victim lies the largest region of the World of Mist. This area contains several exits that you can reach only with winged boots.

Your objectives for quest 6 are the black onyx, fire magic, and the "A" key. The black onyx increases the power of your shield and armor, so you suffer less damage when attacked. Fire magic is a magical weapon, but by this time, you probably have better spells, like thunder or death. The "A" key unlocks the door to the World Tree.

The black onyx is the hardest item to obtain. You must fight through a castle, then defeat both a bat monster and a huge creature with gnashing teeth. Since this guy has no name, I'll refer to him as Jaws.

By now, you've defeated several bat monsters. But Jaws is, as Monty Python would say, something completely different. Here's the trick: go to the left of the room and wait for

Jaws to approach. When he gets close, cream him with your sword. He'll retreat before attacking again, giving you time to prepare for another thrust. This technique requires good timing, but once mastered it serves you well. You'll be seeing more of Jaws later. Doesn't that make your day?

Quest 7

Use the "A" key to open the door to the World Tree branches. Travel to the right and up, to the branch town of Conflate. Somewhere in Conflate is the Ring of Dwarf, which you need to open a special door. Ask around. You'll find it.

In addition to the ring, you must also find the battle helmet. Exit left from Conflate. You have your choice of two doors. One door is all the way to the left, and the other is above you in the next branch.

Try the left-hand door first. In the branch beyond, find and battle another Jaws. He's protecting the battle helmet, so you have to fight him. This time the fight is tougher, since you don't have a platform to stand on. As he approaches, leap up and hit him. Once again, the timing is tricky. Practice.

When you have the battle helmet and the Key of Dwarf, exit through the second locked door. Beyond, you'll begin quest 8.

Quest 8

First, find the branch town of Daybreak. This will be your base of operations as you search for the objectives of quest 8—the battle suit and the hourglass. The battle suit, together with the helmet, gives the ultimate protection. You'll need it in order to defeat the Evil One.

The hourglass stops time, giving you the power to freeze the enemy and get yourself out of trouble.

Explore the branches around Daybreak carefully. You'll need keys to open some doors. The door to the east of Daybreak opens with the Ring of Dwarf, which you got in Conflate. That door leads to the Town of the Evil Place, better known as Dartmoor.

Quest 9

Dartmoor is the last town you'll visit. Take advantage of its shops to stock up on supplies, especially red potions. West of

Dartmoor lies the fortress, where your ultimate objective, the Evil One, waits.

But before you can approach the Evil One, you must locate the Demon's Ring (which will open the door to the final castle) and Dragon Slayer (the most powerful weapon in the game). You'll find several castles, small and large, in the areas around Dartmoor. You'll need the Demon Ring to open the door of one of the castles. To get the Demon Ring, you must win Dragon Slayer from the King of the Dwarfs.

Look for the king in the largest castle. The rooms in this maze-like structure have many exits, and you must try them all. Make a map.

When you track down the king, you'll discover that he has magically transformed himself into a giant flying lizard. To beat him, you must be fleet of foot and have a good supply of red potion. The dwarf king is one of the toughest hombres in the game, so don't be disappointed if you can't beat him on the first try.

When Dragon Slayer is in your possession, look for a guru. He has the ring.

Quest 10

With Dragon Slayer in hand, find the Evil One and bring an end to his reign of terror. The Demon's Ring opens the last door, providing access to the Evil One's fortress. It's absolutely essential that you map this intricate area. Not only do the rooms have many exits, but the exits don't always lead where you think they would. On your map, mark every possible exit from every room. Then, one by one, try them all. Sooner or later you'll find the Evil One.

Just like the dwarf king, the Evil One is one tough cookie. Before you get into it with him, make sure you have your fill of the red juice. The battle is hard, but you can put this guy out of commission. Death to the Evil One!

Castlevania II: Simon's Quest

Company: *Konami*
Type: *Horror Adventure*

The Game

Objective: To locate and destroy the five remaining pieces of Count Dracula's body.

Organization: The game includes six towns, six mansions, and the arcade-type scenes (forests, swamps, caves, etc.) that connect them. All areas are shown in a side view, with horizontal, and sometimes vertical, scrolling.

Creatures: Minor enemies include vampire bats, ravens, zombies, mummies, wolves, gargoyles, mud men, and others. You must also defeat several boss creatures, including Grim Reaper, Vampira, and Count Dracula himself.

General Strategy: As with most adventure games, pay careful attention to all clues. Keep in mind, though, that some clues are meant to confuse rather than help. This is more a puzzle game than an arcade game, so think about what you're doing. Entrances to some areas are shrewdly hidden.

The Controls

Move left or right.
Go up or down stairs.
Press ↑ to enter a door.
Press ↓ to squat.
Select weapons and items from weapons screen.

Attack with whip.
Press both A and B for a jump attack.
Press B to talk with villagers.

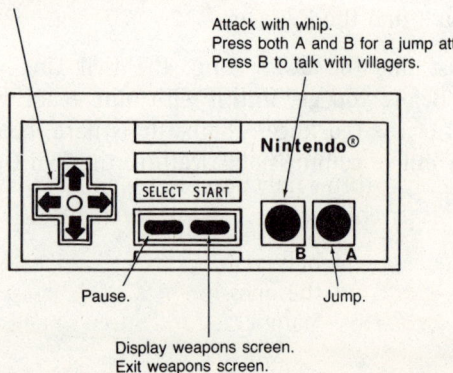

Pause.
Display weapons screen.
Exit weapons screen.
Jump.

The Challenge

I love horror, and I'm not afraid to admit it. If you popped in on me unexpectedly, you'd likely catch me buried in the latest Stephen King novel or perched wide-eyed before the TV, watching a videotape of the newest fearfest from Wes Craven. Sue me. I love the stuff. My idea of the Great American Novel is Clive Barker's *The Great and Secret Show*, and it's beyond me how the movie version of the *The Shining* avoided winning an Oscar for *something*.

Of the creepy-crawly things that inhabit the night, vampires are my favorite. Can't get enough of those fangs, you know? Unfortunately, video games based on these wonderful nocturnal hunters are as rare as roaches in a Raid factory. But they do exist. Three hurrahs, Konami, for *Castlevania* and *Castlevania II: Simon's Quest*. I can't wait for number III.

Strategies

Although *Simon's Quest* contains a good helping of arcade action, the arcade scenes exist only as a method by which to increase your level and earn hearts. At its core, this is a puzzle game. The fastest reaction time and most keenly developed hand/eye coordination in the galaxy won't help you beat the Count. You must gather the clues that will lead you to the five missing parts of Count Dracula's body.

Talk to everyone. And don't just read what they say; write it down. You may think you'll remember the clues; you won't.

Once you've gathered a list of new clues, read them over. Chances are good that they'll tell you what to do next. Remember, though, that a few townspeople lie. Some hints lead nowhere.

In addition to helpful townspeople, the villages also contain secret shops in which you can purchase such essential items as garlic, laurels, holy water, and whips. When a shop seems empty, throw holy water at the floor and walls. You may find a secret entrance.

Speaking of holy water, throw it on every stone block you pass, not just the ones in shops. This is especially important in mansions. Many clues and special items are hidden in stone blocks.

The most important locations in *Castlevania II* are the Berkeley, Rover, Brahm's, Bodley, and Laruba mansions. In each is hidden one of Dracula's body parts, as well as a number of scrolls containing important clues. Once you've visited the mansions and obtained all of the body parts, you'll be ready for Dracula's castle, where your final battle waits.

Your game play should follow this basic pattern:

- Get to a new town.
- While it's daylight, talk to the townspeople. Find all of the shops and see what they're selling.
- When night falls, battle Dracula's minions and gather hearts.
- When daylight returns, go shopping. If you don't have enough hearts to buy what you need, leave town and fight monsters until you do.
- Find the next town or go to the next mansion.

Now let's take a more detailed look at *Castlevania II*.

The Town of Jova

You begin in the town of Jova. Buy two crucial items here—the white crystal and the holy water. Also available in Jova is the thorn whip. After you've talked to all of the townspeople (and written down all their clues), fight some monsters. When you're rich enough, buy the stuff you need.

The Town of Veros

Exit Jova from the right and keep going, through Jova woods and over South Bridge. When you come to Veros Woods, take the low road to Veros.

In Veros be sure to upgrade your equipment by buying a dagger and a chain whip. Don't have enough hearts? Guess you'll have to do some more fighting.

The Town of Aljiba

Exit left from Veros, climb the stairs, and then go right. Continue on past Berkeley Mansion, through Denis Woods and across Dabi's Path. After Aljiba Woods, you'll find the town.

First, locate a friend and exchange your white crystal for a blue one. Then, find laurels, which make you temporarily invincible, and garlic, which encourages some Transylvanians to be more helpful. Leave only when you have a supply of both.

Camilla Cemetery

If you've studied the clues carefully, you know that there's something special about this place. Remember that garlic does amazing things in Transylvania. Use it here, and get a silver knife.

Berkeley Mansion

Dracula's rib is located in Berkeley mansion. To get there, walk left from Aljiba. When you enter Berkeley Mansion, you'll face your first puzzle. How do you get past the entrance? Maybe the blue crystal can help.

Berkeley Mansion is large and complex. It takes a while to learn its layout. While exploring, throw holy water around, or you may miss several scrolls hidden in stone blocks.

When you're finished exploring, buy the oak stake, then find the glowing ball that contains Dracula's rib.

Yuba Lake

Once you have the silver knife and the blue crystal, go to Yuba lake, where a secret passage awaits your discovery. To get to Yuba lake, go down the steps before the town of Aljiba. Where's the secret passage? Have you written down all the clues? Do you remember something about kneeling? Are you tired of all these silly questions?

Rover Mansion

Beneath Yuba Lake you'll find Rover Mansion, a place known for its deadly false floors and mirage walls. As you explore, throw holy water everywhere. Not only will you discover two new clues, but you'll also learn that some walls are not what they seem to be. (If a bottle of holy water passes through a wall without breaking, you can go through the wall too.)

Before you try for the next part of Dracula's body, don't forget to buy an oak stake. You'll find the seller standing on a dangerous, spike-covered floor. Warning: the stone floor above the spikes looks solid enough, but trap doors will drop you down on the spikes. Ouch! Simon on a stick!

Once you have the oak stake, find Dracula's heart.

The Dead River

To get to the Dead River, exit left from Jova (the town in which you start the game) and go through Belasco Marsh. At the river, show the ferryman a part of Dracula's body. Which part you show depends on where you want to go. The first time through, you'll probably want to show him the rib. The second time, the heart.

The Town of Aldora

If you cross the Dead River using the rib, you'll wind up in Aldora. Here, you can stock up on laurels and garlic. More importantly, you can exchange your blue crystal for a red one. While you're in town, speak with everyone. You'll get a couple of false clues here, but they're so ridiculous, you'll recognize them when you hear them. (Dig a hole in a cliff with your head? Sheesh!)

Storigoi Cemetery

After exiting left from the town of Aldora, you'll come to a stairway that leads down to Storigoi Cemetery. Go to the cemetery before you enter Brahm's mansion; a friend has something that will help you survive a tough battle. Summon your friend with garlic.

Brahm's Mansion

Like the other mansions, Brahm's Mansion contains hidden scrolls and someone who will sell you an oak stake. What makes Brahm's Mansion unusual is that it's the home of the Grim Reaper. Sound scary? He is!

The Grim Reaper owns the golden knife. To get it, you must battle him to the death. You better have a good supply of laurels; otherwise, you're in for it.

When you have the golden knife, exit right from the Grim Reaper's room. There's Dracula's eyeball! (Yechhh.) After you get the eyeball, the Grim Reaper comes back. Don't fight this time. Run past him.

The Wasteland

After exiting Brahm's Mansion, go left toward the wasteland. To get there, you'll have to execute several tricky jumps from moving blocks. This feat of dexterity is frustrating at first, but keep trying. Comfort yourself with the knowledge that you need to do this only once.

At the wasteland, a friend will have a diamond for you.

The Town of Andole

Remember the stairs that lead down to Storigoi Cemetery? If you continue to the left, rather than going down those stairs, you'll come to the town of Andole. Here, in addition to doing your usual clue gathering, trade your weapon for a morning star. Get a refill on laurels.

Deborah Cliff

Continue left from the town of Andole, and you'll find the Jam Wasteland. In this area, you must do more leaping from moving stones, after which you'll arrive at Deborah Cliff. If you kneel with the right items, a tornado will sweep you away and deliver you to Bodley Mansion. What a strange world.

Bodley Mansion

Inside Bodley mansion there are more false walls and trap doors than craters on the moon. Watch your step. And whenever you think you've come to a dead end, throw holy water. You might break away some blocks. You might even discover that the blocks are only mirages. Buy your oak stake; then find Dracula's nail.

The Uda Path

When you leave Bodley Mansion, travel left until you come to a lake. Although you can't cross the lake, there's a secret pathway beneath. You know what to do, right? Make sure you have the red crystal.

Beneath the lake is Uda Path, which leads to a strange cavern filled with floating skulls and destructible walls. Use holy water to get past dead ends. Search everywhere. You'll find someone who will upgrade your morning star to the flame whip.

When you have the flame whip, exit left from the caverns. You'll soon get to . . .

Laruba Mansion

Laruba Mansion is the home of Vampira, the malevolent boss demon from whom you must obtain the magic cross. As you search for Vampira, find two friends. One will sell you an oak stake. The other will give you (free!) a supply of laurels.

With laurels in hand, enter Vampira's room. When she weeps her tears of fire, use the laurels for protection. Attack when she circles the room—jump and hit her each time she passes. When she starts weeping again, use the laurels. Continue this pattern until she's dead.

After obtaining the magic cross, exit right. Dracula's ring is yours!

Count Dracula's Castle

Here you are, ready at last for the final confrontation. Your task—bring Dracula's body parts to his castle and destroy him once and for all.

To get to Dracula's castle, exit right from Laruba Mansion, returning the way you came. Head back up the stairs to the lake. From there, go right through two towns (fill up on laurels), until you get to a staircase leading down. Take the staircase and continue right.

Finding Dracula is easy; the castle is small and holds no unfamiliar obstacles. Once you get to Dracula's room, the five body parts come together, and the Count comes back to life. Use your laurels during the fight.

Defeat the Count, and you can put another notch on your controller pad.

Ultima: Exodus

Company: *FCI*
Type: *Role-Playing Adventure*

The Game

Objective: To destroy Exodus.

Organization: The game is set in Sosaria, displayed on your screen as a large scrolling map. During your quest, you'll explore mountains, forests, and oceans, as well as towns and caves. Each cave contains a huge three-dimensional maze with eight levels. In each town, you'll find several shops where you can buy groceries, weapons, armor, tools, and other items.

Creatures: Monsters in Sosaria vary in strength and ability. You'll meet a wide variety of meanies, including orcs, giants, gargoyles, wyverns, goblins, golems, pirates, dragons, sea serpents, and devils.

General Strategy: At first, explore the countryside. Find cities and battle enemies to earn gold and gain experience. Know the strengths and weaknesses of each member of your party. Learn your spells. If you don't use spells properly, you have little chance of surviving. As you get stronger, explore farther and farther from Lord British's castle, gathering clues and purchasing valuable equipment.

The Controls

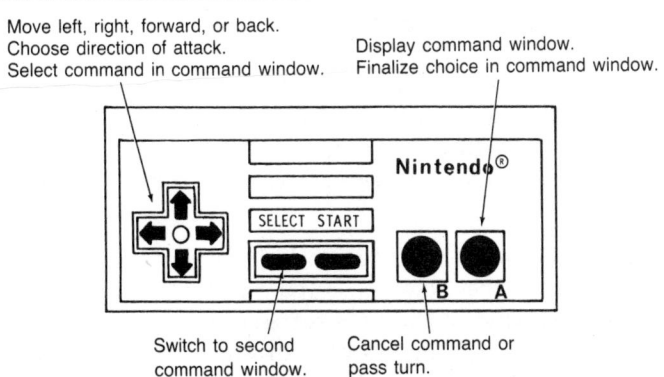

Move left, right, forward, or back.
Choose direction of attack.
Select command in command window.

Display command window.
Finalize choice in command window.

Switch to second command window.

Cancel command or pass turn.

The Challenge

FCI, the makers of *Ultima*, have a slogan. "Not just kid stuff," they say. They're serious. *Ultima* is *Dragon Warrior* all grown up. In fact, it may be the most challenging game available for the Nintendo Entertainment System. When you plug in this cartridge, be prepared to use your noggin and spend many hours unraveling the mystery of Exodus.

Strategies

When you first form your party, put together a good balance of characters. Most importantly, make sure you have the ability to use both the will-power and magic-power systems of magic. I suggest including a cleric and a wizard in every group; the remaining two characters should be strong fighters. The cleric is especially important, due to his healing abilities. In any case, before choosing the members of your party, study the characteristics of each race and occupation. Once you have your group assembled, you can't change without starting completely over.

As in most adventure games, exploration is the key to success. The special items and secrets you need are strewn across Sosaria, and the only way to get them is to travel from town to town (and cave to cave) to search them out.

You'll quickly discover that staying alive takes all the know-how and strategy you can muster. For this reason, save your game frequently. With your game data tucked safely into your cartridge's chips, you can experiment freely, without risking all you've gained.

As you explore, watch your food level closely. If you don't feed your guys, they start dying of starvation. When you arrive in a new town, find the grocery store (if there is one) and stock up. Be aware that your food decreases more rapidly on the Sosaria map than it does in a town or cave. Never have less than 10 units of food per adventurer. For long trips, you need much more.

As you travel, you'll be attacked. Luckily, enemies appear on the map as they advance, so you can avoid them . . . sometimes. Each class of enemy is represented by its own graphic figure. Learn which figures go with which enemy class, then avoid the stronger ones when you can.

As always, talk to everyone, and keep a log of what you're told. At some point in the game, you'll want to review the hints you've gathered. Don't rely on your memory.

Finally, as you explore, make a simple map, noting where each town is and what shops it contains. A good adventure logbook will keep you from having to backtrack.

Fighting

Fighting is unavoidable, so learn to do it well. You need to consider several strategies, not the least of which is your adventurers' battle order. Generally, keep your strongest fighters in front. (Use the order command to rearrange your party if necessary.) When an enemy closes in, the front row is the first to be hit.

Eventually, you'll buy better weapons, some of which you can throw or shoot. Use long-range weapons (including magic) in the beginning of a battle, to weaken attackers before they get close.

Long-range attacks are effective from both the front or rear. However, once the enemy gets close, your front line must take the brunt of the attack. Don't make them face an enemy horde alone. Move at least one of your rear fighters forward.

Having to move characters forward creates a dilemma —should you move or attack on any given turn? You can't do both. Choose your strategy based on the enemies' number and attack formation. In any case, the front-line characters can stay put and enjoy efficient use of their magic and long-range weapons. Thank heavens!

Moving rear characters to the front also allows them to earn experience points more readily. Your characters should advance in experience at the same rate. If one member falls behind, it may be impossible for him to catch up. He'll be forced to confront enemies too strong for him to beat. Some characters, especially strong fighters, tend to earn experience faster than others. You must remedy this. Have a higher-level character weaken an enemy; then let a lower-level character deliver the killing blow and collect the experience.

Some enemies are thieves as well as fighters—they'll steal your gold and supplies. For that reason, it's a good idea to let one member of your party carry all gold and special items. When you meet thieves, keep that character back from the action, where your supplies will be safe.

Did you include a character with healing powers in your party? Smart move. Let no turn pass without healing someone. Unused magic is wasted. You can ignore this rule only when your party is completely healed (rare), when your healer is fighting, or when your healer has too few magic points to cast the spell.

Spells such as Undead or Repel are powerful weapons when used against the right enemies. Use the Undead spell against ghouls and skeletons. Use the Repel spell against orcs and goblins. Know which of your characters can cast these spells, and use them at the beginning of battle. Sometimes, one spell can wipe out an entire enemy force. Strong magical attacks not only indirectly reduce injuries, they also build experience points in a hurry.

The Moon Gates

See that little chart in the upper-left corner of your screen, the one that shows two waxing and waning moons? If you've been wondering what that's for, read on.

Throughout Sosaria are portals called moon gates. When you step into a moon gate, you are transported instantly to another location. Totally awesome, eh? Unfortunately, moon gates are difficult to find because they continually appear and disappear according to the phases of Sosaria's moons. That mysterious chart we were talking about is a moon-gate time table. The chart's left-hand moon controls when a gate opens; the chart's right-hand moon controls where you end up after you enter a gate.

As I said, the gates constantly appear and disappear and so are difficult to find. Most Nintendo Master Gamers discover them only by accident. However, because you had the wisdom and good taste to buy this book, you don't have to rely on chance. I'm going to give you a crash course on locating and using moon gates. Send all thank-yous to me in care of the publisher. Cash only; no checks or credit cards accepted.

Moon gates, when they appear, look like tornadoes viewed from above. When you find one, note the phases of the two moons, then step into the gate. In your notebook, record the moon phases and the place where you end up. Keep in mind that a single gate can transport you to any one of several places, depending on the phase of the right-hand moon. Yeah, I know. It's confusing. Don't toss up your hands and say the heck with it. The only way to some areas of Sosaria is through the moon gates. You *must* find them.

Now, let me guide you to the first gate. When you've found it, you'll be able to locate the others—one gate always leads to another.

The main gate (I call it the main gate because it's the easiest to find) is located near the city of Montor West. Travel west from the city, passing through a forest, until you find a small range of mountains shaped like a short corridor. Stay in that area until the gate appears.

How can you advance time while you're waiting? An easy way is to repeatedly select the Talk command. Each time you select this command, the game's timer advances, and so too do the phases of the moons. Remember, though, that your party members consume food just as if they were exploring. Hungry little devils—bring sufficient supplies.

Sailing the Seven Seas

Okay, maybe there aren't seven. I didn't count. However, the seas of Sosaria, whatever their number, provide access to several cities and caves that you can reach only by ship. (Well, a couple can be reached using moon gates, but you know what I mean.) Early in the game, ships are as rare as cats at a dog show. But as you progress, they appear in ever-increasing numbers.

To get a ship, wait until it docks on the coast. Then approach it as you would a band of enemies. You'll enter the fight mode, and the ship's occupants will attack. Sailors are easier to fight than other creatures, because they attack from two gangways. Keep these swabbies on the gangways, and you'll face no more than two enemies at a time. Wipe out the sailors. Then board the ship.

Just like the countryside, oceans are fraught with danger. Watch for sea serpents, which attack with fireballs, and the powerful Man-of-Wars, which possess deadly magic. Also, avoid other ships, unless you want to fight more enemy sailors.

Have you seen a whirlpool? The whirlpool will take you to Ambrosia, the island home of the shrines of Strength, Dexterity, Intelligence, and Wisdom. In addition, flowers, which you'll need later, grow on Ambrosia.

If Ambrosia is not on your travel plan, avoid the whirlpool.

The Cities

There are eleven cities in Sosaria. Each contains shops where you can buy supplies. You'll also meet many people who can tell you some interesting bits of news. Stop and chat. Each city is unique. Find and visit them all.

If you need help locating the cities or think you're missing something important, read the following paragraphs—each gives a detailed look at one of Sosaria's towns.

Lord British's Castle

The game starts at Lord British's Castle. Here you can visit the inn to save your game or go to the hospital to get cured. In the throne room, the king rewards worthy warriors by increasing their levels.

Lord British's Castle contains many hidden rooms, but you'll need magic keys to get in. Buy these at the guild shop.

In the castle, find, among other things, a fortune teller, a ship, and a treasure room. The fortune teller charges from 100 to 900 gold pieces per clue. The prices seem steep, but it's worth it—you'll need the information to solve the mystery of Exodus.

The Royal City

A short jaunt from Lord British's Castle is the Royal City. Here, you'll find a pub, a weapons shop, an armory, and a grocery store, everything four growing heroes need. Early in the game, you should return to this town often to restock on food and to purchase better weapons. Have a few drinks at the pub. The bartender's stories can be interesting.

When exploring a town like Royal City, check everywhere for clues. Search all forests, as well as the areas outside the city's gates. A townsperson with important information may be anywhere. For example, in Royal City, if you search carefully, you'll meet a young lady who's fond of flowers. Bring her a bouquet, and she will give you a valuable item.

The City of Montor East

Montor East, one of the twin cities, is located south of Lord British's Castle. Here you'll find a weapons shop, an armory, and a pub. As always, helpful citizens have tales to tell. Some important people are hard to find, though. Search everywhere, especially in out-of-the-way places, including outside the city wall.

The City of Montor West

The other twin city, Montor West, is also south of Lord British's Castle, on the other side of the river from Montor East. Here you'll find an armory, a weapons shop, two pubs, a grocery store, and a jail. Prisoners and guards may have important information, and some guards can be bribed, once you've earned the Bribe command. Get that command by talking to a special person in the City of Devil Guard. Hint: Ask more than once for information.

The City of Grey

The City of Grey is near the shore southwest of Lord British's Castle. Grey is a small city, but it's important because it contains a guild shop where you can buy helpful items such as torches, gems, magic keys, and tents. In addition, Grey boasts a grocery store, a weapons shop, an armory, a pub, and a casino. In the casino, try your luck at the children's game, Paper-Scissors-Rock.

Somewhere in Grey is hidden a stash of treasure chests. Bribe a guard.

The City of Moon

Travel west from Lord British's castle, and you'll come upon the City of Moon. Although you can't get weapons or other battle paraphernalia in this peaceful burg, you can visit its grocery store, hospital, pub, or temple. The temple is especially important since you can bring the dead members of your party back to life here, even if a hospital resurrection was unsuccessful. This service costs 900 gold pieces, but your guys are worth it.

As always, search everywhere, and speak to everyone.

The City of Death Gulch

Located on an island southeast of Lord British's Castle, Death Gulch can be reached only by ship or moon gate. Because Death Gulch was cut from the mountains, finding its buildings means traversing maze-like mountain paths. Just getting into this heavily guarded city is a challenge. A maze just below the main gate offers the easiest access, although you still need a magic key to get into the city proper.

Death Gulch contains a weapons shop, an armory, a grocery store, and a pub. The armory holds a cache of treasure chests. If you steal gold, however, plan to battle angry guards. The compass heart is helpful here: once you gather the treasure, you'll want to return quickly to Lord British's Castle. Never heard of the compass heart? Did you bring flowers to a girl in Royal City?

There are four mazes to explore in Death Gulch, as well as several major roads. Townspeople have valuable information. Find everyone. One townsperson, the Priest of Fire, stands in a lava bed. You need the Mark of Fire to get to him safely.

The City of Devil Guard

Situated in a lake surrounded by mountains, this island city can be reached by way of the moon gates. In addition to the pub, hospital, and guild shop, Devil Guard contains a stable where you can buy horses. They're expensive, but they quickly get you where you're going, conserving food and helping you avoid monsters.

The hospital in Devil Guard holds a special secret. With a little prodding, a girl here will give you the Bribe command. Bribing guards is a great way to get into places where you're not supposed to be.

The City of Dawn

This magical city is the toughest to find. Not only is it hidden deep in the woods south of Lord British's Castle, it only appears when both of Sosaria's moons are new. Happy hunting. (Snicker, snicker.)

The City of Dawn offers every type of service, except a casino. There's a weapons shop, an armory, a guild shop, a stable, an inn, a hospital, a grocery store, a fortune teller, and a pub. Whew! A lot of stuff for a small place. Also in Dawn you'll find the golden pick, a special item you need in order to find the magic armor.

Important clues can be gleaned from the people of Dawn. Did you hear about the Lord of Time? About the cards?

The City of Fawn

Get a ship and sail the north seas to the City of Fawn. On this tiny island, you'll find a guild shop, a pub, a casino, a hospital, and a grocery store. There's not much to do here except gather clues. Get information about the Circle of Light, the silver pick, and the Mark of the Snake.

The City of Yew

West of Lord British's Castle, hidden in a forest surrounded by mountains, lies the City of Yew. The buildings in this city are completely enclosed by trees, so they're difficult to find. Explore more carefully than ever before, both for buildings and for townspeople with clues.

Yew offers many shops and services, including a temple, a chapel, and the mysterious Circle of Light. If you've received the Mark of Fire, get the pray command from a priest. Pray in the Circle of Light, and you'll be given an important item, without which you cannot complete the game.

The Caves

Sosaria contains seven caves, each of which is a three-dimensional maze with eight levels. It's impossible to explore them successfully without some careful map-making, so get out your adventure log and a sharp pencil.

Besides being huge, the caves are filled with traps, invisible doorways, ladders, fountains, treasure chests, and, of course, monsters. In addition, special items, such as the silver pick, and the elusive Mark of the King, Mark of Fire, Mark of Force, and Mark of Snake, are hidden throughout.

Getting around in the mazes is tricky at best. Myriad twists and turns make it easy to get lost. To complicate matters, in order to move from one level to the next, you must locate ladders or use spells. Spells are the easiest method, but casting them consumes your magic energy.

Like the cities, each cave is unique. To learn the details, read the following paragraphs.

Golden Cave

This maze is in the mountains east of Lord British's Castle. Within, find the Mark of the King and the Mark of Fire, as well as fountains that heal or poison you. One area contains a lot of gold, but it's difficult to get to.

Each level of Golden Cave has ladders, but they may not always lead where you want to go. There are several hidden doorways (not as many as in the other caves) that you can find by trying to walk through walls. Watch out for the strange wind, which blows out your light. Even magical light is affected.

A fountain on level 2 completely restores your characters' hit points. Find it first, then return to it throughout the game for a quick heal.

Death Cave

Just north of Lord British's Castle, Death Cave contains the silver pick. It also contains the Mark of the King and lots of fountains, treasures, traps, and monsters. Hidden doors abound, especially in level 3, where the important items (treasures and healing fountains) can be reached only through the hidden doorways.

Cave of Sol

Located on a small island southeast of Lord British's Castle, the Cave of Sol can be reached by ship or moon gate. Most of the fountains here are poisonous. At least one fountain restores hit points, if you can find it. Secret doors are everywhere and provide access to areas that you can reach no other way. Look for the Mark of Fire and the Mark of Snake.

Blazing Fire Cave

Blazing Fire Cave lies in the mountains southeast of Lord British's Castle. Inside, you'll find the Mark of Fire and the Mark of Force. Unfortunately, you'll also find plenty of traps.

The important stuff is tucked way down on the eighth level. That figures, right?

The ladders are hard to find, since one ladder rarely connects with another. Secret doors add to the confusion. A room filled with treasure in the northeast corner of level 1 is fairly easy to get to—if you find the right secret doors.

Cave of Fools

The Cave of Fools is in the far south on a peninsula west of Montor West. In addition to scattered treasure chests and fountains, this maze's main feature is the Mark of Force, which, of course, is on level 8. Locating the stairways in this dungeon requires patience, since some levels are extremely complicated. A strange wind will extinguish your light, leaving you fumbling in pitch blackness. Not afraid of the dark, are you?

Cave of Madness

If you've explored many caves, you're probably already just a step from a stay at the Institute for the Potentially Nervous. Trust me—the Cave of Madness is the last thing you need. Located on the central west coast of Sosaria, the Cave of Madness owes its name to its many isolated rooms containing only ladders. Choose the wrong ladder, and you'll climb, cursing and whining, from one dead end to the next.

Here's a little help: To get quickly to the Mark of Fire, take the ladder at the entrance all the way down to level 8. If you explore other areas, you can find the Mark of the King, as well as gold and fountains. You can reach the main rooms of Level 2 only with a descend or sink spell; the ladders there pass directly through to lower levels.

Have fun!

Cave of Moon

Find this important maze on an island just east of Death Gulch. Use a moon gate to get there. In this dungeon, get the

Mark of the King and the Mark of Fire. Look for a king with important information.

Not surprisingly, all the goodies are on level 8. You can get down to level 8 quickly, though, once you locate the ladder in the very southeast corner of level 1. Those who like to explore can find treasure as well as fountains for recovering hit points. You can also find traps, monsters, and dead ends. Be my guest.

Ambrosia

During your ocean travels, you've undoubtedly noticed a whirlpool. This rare ocean phenomenon is the gateway to a strange but important island called Ambrosia. Here you'll find the shrines of Intelligence, Wisdom, Strength, and Dexterity. In addition to the shrines, Ambrosia has some very unusual vegetation. Didn't you meet someone who liked flowers?

Ambrosia is a huge island. To explore it completely requires time and patience, because it's filled with dangerous mountain mazes and savage creatures. The shrines are especially difficult to reach. For example, to get to the Shrine of Dexterity, you must get through a maze in the southwest corner of Ambrosia, fight a band of pirates to get a ship, sail the ship east past dangerous monsters, and disembark in just the right place.

At the shrines, donate 100 gold pieces to increase a character's strength, intelligence, wisdom, or dexterity by one point. Yeah, it's expensive. It's also necessary. You must improve each character's abilities if you plan to survive long enough to meet Exodus. An extra-intelligent wizard, for example, can use more effective spells and recover magic points more quickly. Similarly, a character with additional dexterity hits his target more often, while a character with additional strength can do more damage in battle. Extra wisdom makes clerics (and other users of the will-power system of magic) more powerful. Get the message?

The cards are another important reason to visit the shrines. When you pray at a shrine, you receive one card. Only when you have all four cards, along with the silver horn and the Mark of Snake, can you consider attacking Exodus Castle.

Exodus Castle

At last, the end of your quest.

On Sosaria's southern-most island sits Exodus Castle, its entrance guarded by a giant snake. In order to advance into the castle, you must have all four cards, the silver horn, and the Mark of Snake. In addition, your characters should be at the highest level and have attained maximum abilities. Finally, you should have the magic armor and the mystic sword. Ready?

Exodus Castle is a huge maze filled with evil creatures and dead ends. Expect some nasty surprises. Only the finest warriors can find their way through the castle and defeat Exodus. If you make it, congratulations! You are truly a Nintendo Master Gamer.

Shadowgate

Company: *Seika*
Type: *Graphic Text Adventure*

The Game

Objective: To find and destroy the Warlock Lord.

Organization: The entire game takes place inside Shadowgate Castle. As you move from room to room, the graphic depicting your location changes. Although the scenes are mostly static, some animation is used. The rest of the screen is taken up by the command menu and your inventory.

Creatures: Plan to meet such wonders of nature as dragons, trolls, wraiths, mummies, wyverns, hellhounds, werewolves, and more.

General Strategy: Examine everything, paying careful attention to things that look different or special. Take every object you can; there's no limit to what you can carry. Read all text carefully—you'll find essential clues in the descriptions.

The Controls

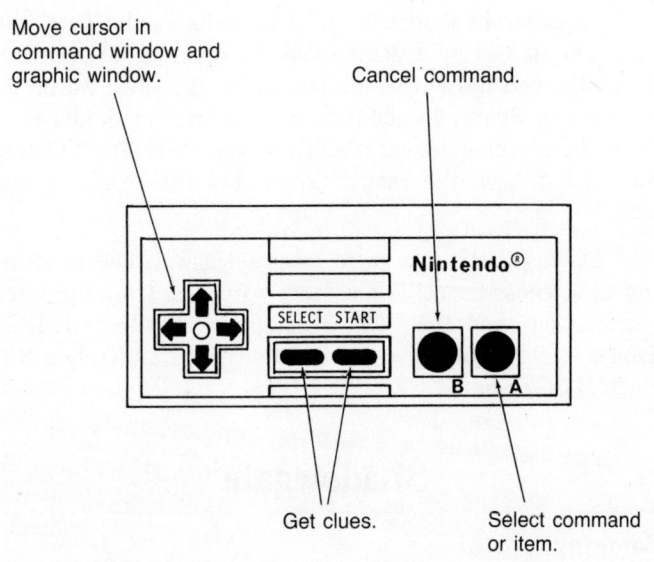

Move cursor in command window and graphic window.

Cancel command.

Get clues.

Select command or item.

The Challenge

Text adventures have long been a staple of computer entertainment. Although they represent one of the first types of computer games, they've never lost popularity. This is probably due to their ability to draw players in, to make them feel as though they're really a part of the game's world. Playing a text adventure is much like reading a book, or being *in* a book. In fact, text adventures are sometimes referred to as *interactive novels*.

A word of warning: *Shadowgate* is difficult. You'll have to brainstorm and look at a problem from several different angles. You'll spend a lot of time staring at the screen, thinking about what to do next. At times, you'll be as perplexed as a moose in a tree. Still, like anything that takes effort, the rewards are great.

Strategies

The basic strategy is to collect objects and determine how to use them. Sound easy? Well, it's not. You'll have to keep track of a lot of objects and use your imagination to figure out how to use them. To complicate matters, some objects can be combined to make new ones, and some have no purpose at all . . . except to confuse you.

When you enter a new room, study it carefully for visual clues. Examine everything. Pay close attention to all textual descriptions. These hints are essential.

Try to pick up every object you see. If you can take something, chances are you'll need it later. *Shadowgate* imposes no limit on the size of your inventory, so take everything.

At first (after you find a certain key), you'll be able to move throughout the castle easily, finding new rooms and picking up new objects. Eventually, however, you'll get stumped. When that happens, scan the objects in your inventory and think of how you can use them. Re-examine every room for clues. You may have missed something.

The Real Help

Being successful at a text adventure means solving a long string of puzzles, each unique in its own way. So rather than the usual strategy guide, below is a list of questions and answers, arranged in the order in which you're likely to need them. If you get stuck, find a question that relates to your problem and read the hint that follows. Mind you, I'm not giving answers, only hints that'll nudge you in the right direction. Use your noodle.

How can I open the second door?

Did you notice the skull outside Shadowgate's entrance?

How can I open the smaller door?

A book might help.

How can I get the objects from the dragon's lair?

One object, if picked up first, will protect you.

How can I get past the landslide next to the waterfall?

You can't, but maybe you can get behind the waterfall.

What should I do in the room with the pedestal?

See the hole in the wall? Put something in it.

How can I get the key from the skeleton?

If you had something cold, you could freeze the water.

Can I retrieve objects from the frozen lake?

Melt the water with something hot.

Am I missing something in the hallway with the book?

Look closely. There's a secret entrance in one of the walls.

Okay, I found the room beyond the secret entrance. Now what?

There's a secret door here, too, and a secret way to open it.

How can I get past the wraith?

Is there something special about one of your torches?

Is there something I should know about the room with the rope?

There's another secret entrance.

What do I do once I find the secret entrance?

Put something into the stone slab.

What do I do with all the coffins?

Open the right ones.

How do I know which are the right ones?

Sheesh! I can't tell you everything. Experiment, but save your game first.

What about the mummy?

It's ancient wrappings are combustible.

What about the mirrors?

Something you have will break them. But don't break the wrong one — it's bad luck.

I can't get into the fire room!

Have you found something you can wear?

Okay, so now I'm in the fire room. I still can't go anywhere.

Put out the fires with something cold.

What's with this troll?

Use the proper weapon on him.

And how about the cyclops?

Same as with the troll. Just make sure he's dead.

Am I supposed to do something with the well?

Bring up the bucket.

Now I'm in the library. Any ideas?

Did you look in the desk?

Any more ideas?

Put something in the hole by the bookcase.

I can't read the book on the desk

Maybe you need something to help you see better.

Can I do anything with the globe?

Have you learned any spells yet?

What do I do in the lab?

Take everything you can. One item you need is hard to see.

Anything else?

How about that different-looking stone in the floor?

I can't get that darn flute!

Wear something to protect your hand.

A flute? What the devil am I supposed to do with a flute?

Play it, of course.

Is there something special about the rug in the banquet hall?

Like most rugs, it's combustible.

How can I answer the riddles?

Use your head. You can answer each riddle by an item you should have in your inventory. If you can't figure out the riddles, see the end of this section.

What about the star map?

There's something on it and something behind it.

Nice looking lady, but she keeps killing me!

Use the proper weapon.

Now I have to deal with a hellhound too?

You should have something that's been blessed. Use it.

Can I defeat the dragon?

Yep. With something you usually see in the sky.

What do I do with the thing that looks like a flag-pole mount?

Put something in it that'll attract lightning.

Is the skeleton of the king special?

Put something in his empty hand.

Hey, neat! I found a secret panel. How do I open it?

Put something in the hole.

How can I cross the broken-down bridge?

Something will make you very light.

What do I do with the giant snake?

Did you find the wand?

Darn! The troll's back!

Try magic.

What do I do in the room with the big hole in the floor?

Try the levers on the right-hand side.

So what? The levers haven't helped me much.

You have to move them in the right order. Do you remember some symbols marked on the wall in the riddle room?

What do I do about the gargoyles?

Try a spell.

I opened the second well, but when I enter it, I die.

The right coin might do the trick.

How do I get a ride from the boatman?

Pay him, of course. Even specters want to be paid for their labors.

What do I do in the room with the three symbols?

Put something into the opening below the sword.

Okay, that worked. Now what?

Do you have another musical instrument?

How can I beat the behemoth?

With the Staff of Ages.

Okay, wise guy, how do I create the Staff of Ages?

Combine the regular staff with two other items.

Hey! The behemoth is gone, and he took the Warlock Lord with him. Now there's a neat story playing across the screen.

Congratulations! You've won the game.

The Riddles

The Sphinx's riddles are fairly difficult, especially if you don't have the right objects in your inventory. (I told you to take everything, didn't I?) If you can't solve a riddle, consult the next paragraph, but *only* if you're really stumped.

For each riddle, give the sphinx one of these objects —the map from the library, the horseshoe from the laboratory, the bellows from the study, the skull from the dragon's cave, the mirror from the banquet hall, or the broom from the mirror room. I won't tell you which object goes with which riddle. That would be too easy.

SCIENCE FICTION

Science Fiction

Bionic Commando

Company: *Capcom*
Type: *Arcade Rescue Mission*

The Game

Objective: To rescue Super Joe and sabotage the Albatross project.

Organization: The game is made up of 19 stages of play, each of which is a horizontally or vertically scrolling scene. A map screen allows you to move from one stage to the next.

Creatures: Most enemies are soldiers, including infantrymen, helicopter pilots, and gunmen. Sometimes, however, you will encounter strange creatures that resemble insects or man-eating plants.

General Strategy: At first, kill as many enemies as you can. Collecting the bullets they leave behind allows you to withstand limited amounts of damage. Most importantly, practice with your bionic arm until you can manipulate it like a master. If you can't use the bionic arm effectively, you have little chance of making it to the final showdown.

The Controls

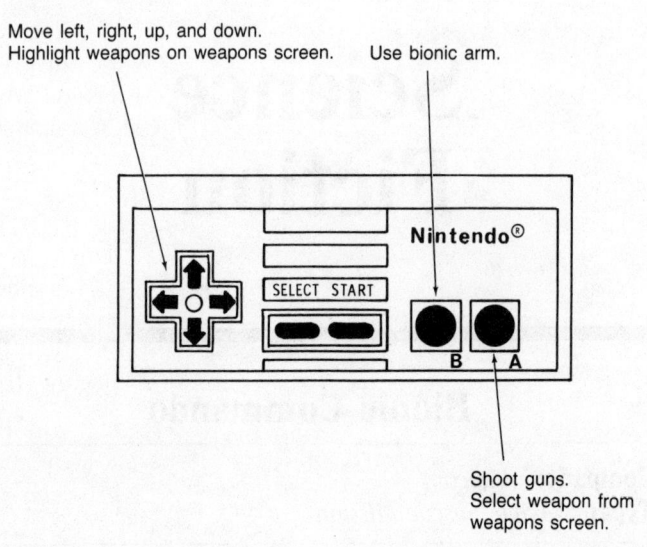

The Challenge

Although *Bionic Commando* contains a lot of arcade action, it's very different from most games of its type. Rather than jumping from place to place, you use a bionic arm to swing and climb from one platform to another, like some futuristic Tarzan. This unique method of moving around the screen sets *Bionic Commando* apart from its competition, making it a game you'll definitely want to add to your collection.

Strategies

Use your bionic arm to climb and swing, always being ready to blast the enemy soldiers. Some soldiers are difficult to get past at first. Learn how they attack—then take them out.

Practice using your bionic arm to swing from one location to another without touching the ground. For example, in some areas you must cross a ceiling by swinging, dropping, and then grabbing the ceiling again before falling. Perfect this move or you'll pay for it later.

Although not mentioned in the manual, *Bionic Commando* does have a continue feature. In fact, with good planning, you can get virtually unlimited continues. How? On the main game map, as you move from one location to another, enemy forces, traveling in trucks, may attack you. When you fight these forces, look for soldiers carrying white shields or driving jeeps. When you kill them, they leave behind white eagle medals. Each medal is worth one continue. Get as many as you can.

Before entering each combat area, you must choose the equipment you want to bring with you. For example, some communicators work only with a specific radio. In addition, some weapons are more useful in some areas than in others. I'll tell you which items I think are best for each section. But don't be afraid to experiment. You might find different items work better for you.

Now let's take a look at each area in detail. We'll study them not in numeric order, but in the order in which you should play them.

Area 1

In area 1, visit the communications rooms in order to gather some helpful hints. Be sure to check both the radio and the wire tap or you won't be able to enter subsequent areas. You'll find two communications rooms. The first is on the top of the first building.

On top of the second building is a door. If this door is closed, you didn't take advantage of both the radio and the wire tap in the first communications room. Write 50 times on the blackboard "I will learn to follow instructions."

Inside the second building, take the elevator down two floors and look for another communications room. Now find the area 1 reactor. Destroying the reactor is a snap. The bad news is you'll have to fight through several soldiers to get to it.

Area 13

Your next stop (after gathering continues as described in the "Strategies" section above) should be area 13—one of the seven Red Cross stations in the game. Here, no one will attack—as long as you behave yourself. Check every doorway. Find a bullet and a flare bomb.

Area 4

Take the flare bomb and enter area 4. Here you'll get a real test of your bionic arm skills as you swing over a series of spiked pits. After surviving the spikes and battling a few guards, you'll see another communications room.

Take care of business in the communications room, then head up to the area 4 control room, where you'll find the next reactor. The guard here shoots with both a gun and a bionic arm. Although his gunshots can injure you, the arm can only knock you around. Shoot out the reactor, and you'll be awarded the wide cannon.

Area 15

Area 15 is another Red Cross station. In the first room grab a one-up, but watch out for the spiked floor! Now head to the right, blasting the wall with your gun and fighting the enemy soldiers. In the second room get the orange radio.

Area 5

Here you need the wide cannon, the energy potion, and the red radio.

Remember, you can't stand on lights, but you can attach your bionic arm to them and pull yourself up. With this in mind, head up to the first communications room.

After reading the messages, continue up. Climb quickly, trying to stay above the helicopters. Hint: If you hit a helicopter with your arm, it may drop down a little . . . into the range of your weapon.

A little farther up, find the next communications room.

After leaving the communications room, move up, using the spring girders. Here's how:

1. Climb, staying to the right, until you get to the first spring girder.

2. Move to the far right of the right-hand girder (you should be standing on it), then face left.
3. Use your bionic arm to grab the bottom of the spring girder. Pull yourself up.
4. When you get on the girder, you'll immediately bounce up. Quickly grab the next girder up.

Use this technique to get to area 5's control room.

In the control room, move right until the robot guard's shots can't reach you. Blast the robot guard and the reactor. Now you've got the rocket launcher.

Area 16

On to area 16, another Red Cross station. Beyond the first door, find the green radio. Beyond the second door, get some obvious, and mostly worthless, advice. Aren't you glad you stopped in?

Area 2

Before entering this area, select the rocket launcher, the energy potion, and the green radio. Now travel to the right and up, avoiding the water. If it gets a grip on you, it'll carry you down a drain like a maple leaf in a flood. At the top find a communications room.

After leaving the communications room, move to the left. You'll come to a vertical shaft. The reactor room is in a short passage on the left of the shaft—getting to it is tricky. Drop off the platform at the top of the shaft and free-fall until you see an opening on the left. Immediately stop your fall by grabbing a platform with your bionic arm. If you miss, you must use your arm to climb back up, a frustrating job that will have you throwing your NES controller at the TV and inventing new words.

When you find the door to the reactor room, don't let the water drag you away again. Fight the soldiers and destroy the reactor. Three shots with your rocket launcher should get you the pendant.

Area 3

In area 3 you need the rocket launcher, the pendant, the energy potion, and the green radio. Use tree limbs to keep from sinking into the snow. When you're on the grassy platforms, watch out for the man-eating plants. They'll crush you into bionic scrap with a single snap of their jaws. Work your way up and to the left. At the top, enter the door.

Swing over to the elevator and ride it down. At the bottom, get on the second elevator. Be prepared. This elevator drops like a carnival ride for the insane. A door appears almost immediately on the left. Grab the left wall. The door leads to a communications room.

Now head out to the corridor on the right, swinging over the guard. When you can go right no farther, drop down and continue left, swinging over some spiked floors. On the far left, find the door to the reactor chamber. Use your rocket launcher to take out the robot guard with one shot. Destroy the reactor and get the rapid fire device.

Area 6

This is one of the toughest levels in the game. Don't enter this level till you've mastered your bionic arm. When you're ready, select the rocket launcher, the pendant, the energy potion, and the green radio. Then descend to area 6.

First, blast out a wall. See that one-up? Unless you're very skillful, don't try to get it. It's not worth the effort.

Head up the first building and move right. Kill the enemies that control the drones. Then, move from the first building to the second, by swinging between the light poles. Hope you have a lot of continues. This maneuver requires practice.

Find a door in the second building, and enter it to get to the third building, where the fun really begins. Your bionic arm can't grip some of the girders here. Other girders are covered with boxes, making it tough to get up to them. Even more interesting, some enemies here roll balls of energy across your path. Having fun yet?

The area 6 control room is at the top of this building. The humanoid robot that guards the reactor is one tough critter. Avoid him. Concentrate on the reactor with your rocket launcher, and you'll soon get the permit.

Area 14

You need the permit to access this Red Cross station, where you can get the blue radio and 10 bullets.

Area 8

Here you need the rocket launcher, the pendant, the energy potion, and the blue radio.

This area is a large maze with many doors and pathways. However, it's easy to move in this area, and that more than makes up for the area's size and complexity. Explore thoroughly, finding and visiting two communications rooms.

Once you've been to the communications rooms, the door to the control room will open. The soldiers here can be shot only from the back. Blast the reactor, and collect the iron boots.

Area 19

This is another Red Cross station, but you'll have to fight enemies here. Worse, all you'll get for your troubles is four bullets and a crazy soldier who begs to be shot. Maybe you should skip this area.

Area 9

Take the rocket launcher, the pendant, the energy potion, and the blue radio before you enter area 9. To get to the main part of the base, you must fall down the narrow pit. However, before you do, swing over the pit and to the right. Hey! A one-up!

Like area 8, area 9 is fairly easy. Visit the communications room on the left. Then head up and to the right. To ride the garbage cars, stand on the track and let a car hit you. You'll suffer some damage, but you'll also bounce up into the car.

At the top of the base, find the reactor room. Fight a few soldiers, destroy the reactor, and collect your reward: the three-way gun.

Area 17

In this Red Cross station, meet two people, only one of whom has anything valuable to say.

Area 7

Ready to rescue Super Joe? Pack the wide cannon, the pendant, the energy potion, and any radio. Then enter area 7. The toughest obstacles here are the jeeps, the two-man helicopters, and the electrical wires you must swing on to get to the reactor room. Handle the jeeps and helicopters with the wide cannon. Then climb up. Move to the left by swinging from the transformers on the wires.

The robot in the area 7 control room is particularly vicious. Stand below him until he's out of your way, then jump up onto his platform for a few quick shots at the reactor. Once the reactor is kaput, you'll have rescued Joe. But, as Joe will inform you, your mission is far from over.

Area 18

This is the last Red Cross station. Look for Destroyer-2 and get the machine gun.

Area 10

Although Super Joe wants you to meet him in area 12, you can't get there yet. So, your next stop is area 10. For this portion of your mission, bring the wide cannon, the pendant, the energy potion, and the orange radio.

After entering area 10, move to the right, blasting the sliding guns as you go. Watch out for the spiked floor on the far right. Get up on the platform that holds two boxes. To climb to the next platform, stand behind the boxes (to the left) and use your bionic arm to swing out to the right. Grab the platform above as you pass beneath it. At the top, go to the left. Avoid the red water.

After crossing a series of platforms, you'll find the communications room. As usual, check out the communicator and wire tap. When you leave the communications room, run immediately to the left, swing from the ceiling above the spiked floor, and land on the moving platform. If you hesitate, you'll fall on the spikes. Can you say bionic pin cushion?

Keep moving left and up until you get to the reactor room, where you'll meet a familiar enemy. Destroy the reactor and collect a one-up.

Area 11

Enter area 11 with the wide cannon, the pendant, the energy potion, and the orange radio. At the beginning of this area is a pit of flames over which several platforms move. Don't use the platforms to get to the other side. Instead, swing from the ceiling. (It'll take several mid-air grabs and swings to make it.) If you fall, the moving platforms will take you back for another try.

After the fire pits, climb up, where you'll find a communications room on the right.

Now, move to the left and perform another series of ceiling swings to get over the second set of fire pits. This area is even tougher than the first. Here are three hints: practice, practice, practice.

On the other side, enter the reactor room. Sliding ceiling guns and a few soldiers are here to greet you. Wipe 'em out. Then you can destroy the reactor without distractions and get the bullet-proof vest.

Area 12

For area 12, the final part of your mission, bring the rocket launcher, the bullet-proof vest, the energy potion, and the orange radio.

Area 12 contains several reactor rooms. When destroyed, one reactor shuts off the force field generators. Another reactor, strangely enough, can't be destroyed at all.

After blasting the reactors, find Albatross, a huge floating machine which you must destroy before you can advance further in the game. Albatross has only one vulnerable area: the glowing orange section of the engine. Use your bionic arm to climb onto the small platform behind the forward-most jet. Slightly above you and to the right is another jet. See it? Use that jet as an anchor for your arm. Swing up and grab the metal to the left of the engine. Hang there and blast away.

Next, find and destroy Master-D's helicopter by dropping off the ledge and blasting the helicopter's cockpit as you fall.

You now have 60 seconds to get off the base before it explodes. Get cranking! On your way out, you'll run into a particularly ornery robot. Don't fight him. Keep climbing.

Did you make it out? Congratulations! Sit back and enjoy the game's ending sequence.

Super C

Company: *Konami*
Type: *Science Fiction Arcade*

The Game

Objective: To battle soldiers and outer-space bosses, until you meet and destroy Red Falcon's closest allies.

Organization: *Super C* consists of eight levels, each of which is displayed in a vertically scrolling, horizontally scrolling, or overhead perspective.

Creatures: This game is packed with strange beasts, mechanical devices, and soldiers (both aliens and brainwashed U.S. GIs). Besides tanks, helicopters, and cannonball launchers, you'll fight such bizarre enemies as the Lip-O-Suction mouths, the Babalu Destructoid Mechanism, and the Krypto-Crustacean.

General Strategy: Practice controlling the angle of your weapon. The terrain changes often, requiring quick attacks in different directions. In addition, anticipate the direction from which your enemies will approach. You'll then have time to prepare. Because you have only one life, play defensively. Specifically, learn to somersault around bullets.

The Controls

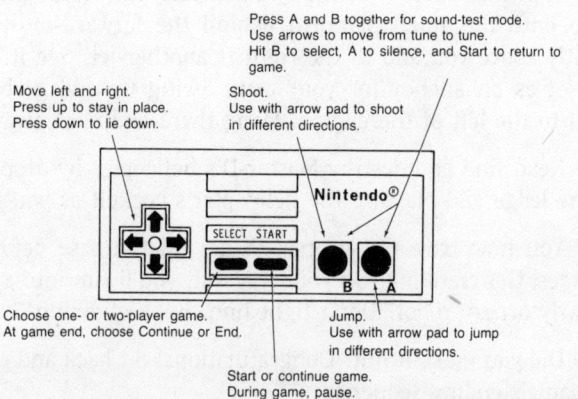

The Challenge

A couple of years ago, Konami released an alien search-and-destroy mission called *Contra*. This exciting arcade blastathon was an immediate hit, thanks to nonstop action and a two-player cooperative mode.

As we all know, successes breed like mice in a drain pipe. This phenomenon, known in medical circles as sequelitis, has been responsible for such "masterpieces" as *Jaws 4, A Nightmare on Elm Street 5, Star Trek 5,* and a long line of *Police Academy* films. Video game makers, too, can fall prey to sequelitis.

This time, we're glad they did.

Strategies

The best weapon, bar none, is the spread gun. Use it whenever you can. You'll live longer.

As you fight, you'll sometimes find a Mega Shell capsule—a bonus item that destroys everything on the screen. Wait as long as you can before grabbing it. The more enemies you can lure onto the screen, the better.

Many enemies sneak up from behind, so watch your back. There's no time limit for each level. Advance carefully.

Watch for the power-up capsules. Shoot them to make them drop to the ground. If you want the capsule's powers, run over it.

Area 1: The Gates of Fort Fire Storm

When traveling uphill, keep your weapon aimed up. Otherwise you'll shoot more ground than enemies. Don't forget, though—soldiers sometimes charge from behind.

Take your time. If you rush into battle, you may run headlong into a grenade or enemy. Move slowly until you learn the enemies' pattern of attack.

At the top of the hill is a helicopter loaded with troops. Destroy the side gun turrets first. Then concentrate on the back door. This stops the soldiers from jumping out. Watch for sneak attacks from the left.

Area 2: The Warped Mind Command Center

When you get to the tanks, hang back and study their attack pattern. Any Nintendo Master Gamer will soon see safe areas from which to battle. Keep in mind that most foes have only a limited attack range. Sit back until their shots are all on screen. When they stop to recharge, attack.

Watch yourself in narrow passages. It's easy to get trapped in a corner by enemy fire.

At the end of this level is a powerful tank, guarded by three gunmen and an electric probe. Stand on the black skirt that leads to the road the tank occupies. (For the most part, this will keep you out of range of its shots.) Take out the two gunmen on either side. The last gunman will continue the attack, but he'll soon give up.

Area 3: The Tropics of Torture

Again, don't rush into battle, or you may fall victim to machine guns that pop up from the ground. In addition, watch out for snipers. They attack from trees and bushes.

In this area you'll face the cannonball launcher. Although you can destroy the globes it shoots before they hit you, concentrate on blasting the machine rather than its shots.

After the water section, you'll come to a gray clearing. Here you'll face the horrible Babalu Destructoid Mechanism (BDM), a walking fortress of devastation. If you stay to the left of the screen, you can do a lot of damage when it first appears. Not enough to destroy it, though. When the BDM gets too close, leap on it and take a ride until it's back on the right side. Then jump off and continue your attack from the left.

Once you've dispatched the BDM, move on to the earthquake zone. Advance a little at a time and be ready to leap to safety if the earth drops out from beneath you.

Finally, you'll take on a machine with four rotating guns. Stand directly under it until it shoots, then go to the left or right until it shoots again, then back to the center. Blast the machine as you dodge. Once you've destroyed one of the guns, it gets easier, but don't let up till you fry it.

Area 4: The Lair of the Jungle

Inside this fortress, you'll face not only another wave of nasties, but also some deadly globes that drop from the ceiling. To get past them, stand toward the left (watching for sneak attacks) and jump while fanning shots at the globes.

You'll come to a room filled with high platforms and gunmen. Don't jump up until all the explosive ceiling tiles have fallen. The lower platform shields you.

In the vertically scrolling scene, pause every few steps to wait for possible attacks by winged enemies. When you get to the rising platform, you'll be faced with pivoting guns mounted on the walls, sliding guns on rails, bubbles that follow you around the screen, and many more winged enemies. You'd better have a cache of men saved up or you won't survive. Use the spread gun and keep moving.

Finally, a saucer that fires deadly rays from nine guns appears above you. Start at the left and aim your fire straight up. Then angle your shots to the right. This attack strategy will wipe out the three left guns. Continue this pattern until the saucer is destroyed. Don't get caught under a gun when it's firing!

Area 5: The Massacre Mountains

In this area, which is similar to the waterfall level in *Contra*, you must leap up on small, craggy ledges packed with turrets and gunmen. To see what's above, jump straight up, so the screen display shifts upward with you. Be careful of platforms that drop off the bottom of the screen. If you land on one, you'll fall with it. Also, watch out for jet-pack soldiers flying up the sides, as well as boulders that drop from above.

When you finally get to flat land, be prepared for a couple of long drops. Falling won't hurt you, but watch out for enemies attacking from behind.

Finally, fight the Krypto-Crustacean. As it drops closer and closer, it throws killer skulls and blazing missiles. The skulls always move toward the center of the screen. The missiles hang in the air before heading for you. Keep moving—avoid standing directly under the Krypto-Crustacean. You don't want it dropping onto your head, do you?

Area 6: Jagger Froid's Fruit-of-the-Doom Defense Line

In this overhead-view battle, you must pick off Jagger Froid's sidekicks, one by one. Look out for the Lip-O-Suction mouths, which will kill you on contact. Figure out where they're about to open and steer around them.

This level is packed with bad guys. Still, it's possible to get through without injury. One enemy, a nasty-looking face, is actually easy to destroy. Stand about three-quarters of the way down the screen and fire straight into the skull. As you're attacking the face, a dragon will emerge from a tube on the side and fly across the screen. If you're in the right place, the dragon will circle around you without mishap and then exit.

Area 7: The Radioactive Lava

This is a wild level, with lots of jumps and drops. Take your time, and keep your distance from the creatures here. On the downhill, if a skeleton attacks from behind, jump over it and then shoot it from above. After cutting through the bubble-like floor, try to stay above the lizard hatchers. Blast them from above, and you're less likely to be killed by their savage offspring. If you must shoot a hatcher from the same platform, keep your distance, so you don't get a faceful of lizard.

The final drop takes you to the Temple of Terror. To beat this strange creature, use carefully timed jumps, and shoot directly up into the Temple's belly. Watch out for the drips and missiles.

Area 8: Red Falcon's Poison

In this, the final level, you'll take on many of Red Falcon's lieutenants. As you advance, avoid the missile spitters, deviously hidden in the terrain. In addition, plan to negotiate some long, strength-sapping jumps. As you move up, watch out for statue heads—they fire some fast-moving bullets.

In one area the ceiling moves down toward you. Don't worry about headroom—at least, not yet. Instead, dispatch the flaming globes that appear. You can't shoot through the ceiling. You must either gun down the globes before the ceiling comes down too far, or outrun them. (Shooting globes under a low ceiling is possible, but difficult.)

Now, see that series of small platforms? Start worrying about headroom. Without it you can't leap high enough to reach the next platform.

Finally, when the walls start crumblin' down, stay to the far left until an underground creature appears. If you stand in front of the creature, its red shots will sail over your head. You can easily disarm the blue shots while you blast its head.

That's it! With the Earth again free of Red Falcon, you can fly off into the horizon for that well-deserved R&R. But if you want your vacation to last, don't answer the door or look at the mail.

MILITARY

Military

Strider

Company: *Capcom*
Type: *Futuristic Rescue Mission*

The Game

Objective: To locate and rescue your friend Kain, then deal with the evil Matic.

Organization: You will travel to Kazakh, Egypt, Japan, Africa, Australia, China, and Los Angeles. In each location is a base you must search, each made up of vertically and horizontally scrolling scenes.

Creatures: In addition to soldiers, various kinds of automated weapons will do their best to keep you from infiltrating the bases. Boss soldiers include Badger, Dragon Friend, Kodiak, and Flash Blade, to name a few.

General Strategy: Search everywhere. Many items, including six computer disks and three types of boots, are essential to complete the game. Friends who will give you important information or helpful items are also hiding in the bases. Don't leave any area unexplored.

The Controls

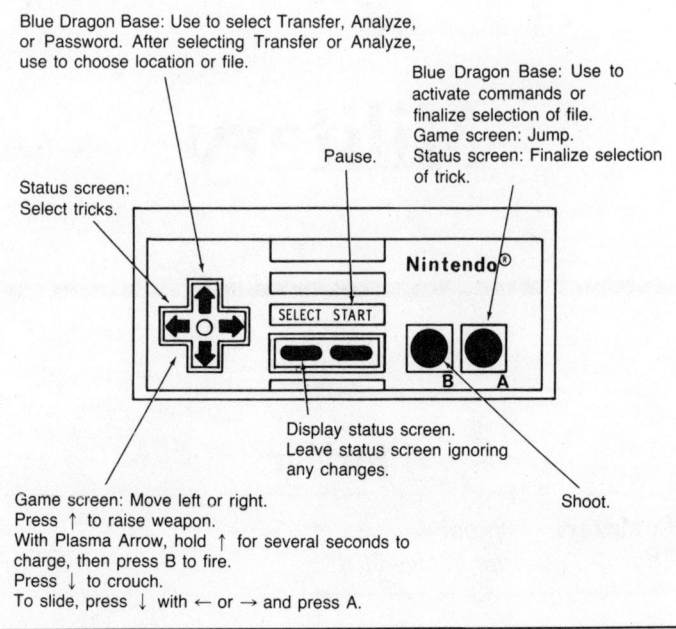

Blue Dragon Base: Use to select Transfer, Analyze, or Password. After selecting Transfer or Analyze, use to choose location or file.

Status screen: Select tricks.

Pause.

Blue Dragon Base: Use to activate commands or finalize selection of file.
Game screen: Jump.
Status screen: Finalize selection of trick.

Display status screen. Leave status screen ignoring any changes.

Shoot.

Game screen: Move left or right.
Press ↑ to raise weapon.
With Plasma Arrow, hold ↑ for several seconds to charge, then press B to fire.
Press ↓ to crouch.
To slide, press ↓ with ← or → and press A.

The Challenge

Strider's biggest asset is the interesting world in which it's played. The graphics are handsome, intriguing, and full of detail. Although it's a short game with little depth, it contains enough of a challenge to make it a good play.

Strategies

None of the objects—files, boots, keys, etc.—are hard to find. Search everywhere, and you can't help but stumble upon them. It might help to draw a simple map in order to keep track of the areas you've explored. If you don't examine all areas thoroughly, you might overlook some objects, even if they're not hidden.

   Invisible energy capsules are hidden throughout the bases. Use your weapon to blast all the walls. Finding these capsules can make the difference between losing a life and going on to victory. Be careful, though. You may uncover a bottle of poison—if you pick it up, you'll lose energy.

Except for the boss soldiers, most enemies in *Strider* are wimps. If you've had previous arcade-action experience, these pathetic adversaries will put no blisters on your trigger finger. The boss soldiers are more challenging; a couple even qualify as toughs. Learn their moves, however, and they'll go down easy.

Although *Strider* isn't divided into levels as such, there are areas, numbered S-1 through S-5, which you can enter only with the appropriate key. Some areas remain inaccessible until near the end of the game. Be patient.

When you find a new computer disk, bring it to the Blue Dragon Console to analyze it. Analyzing the computer disks is the only way to get passage to different countries.

Kazakh

Begin your assignment in Kazakh, an area you will often return to as you advance in the game. A guard on the roof will give you key 1. Besides the key, the left side of this base has little to offer. Explore if you like. While you're at it, practice fighting the enemy. When your curiosity is satisfied, move to the right, over the spiked floor and into the right side of the base, where you'll get files 1 and 2.

Return to the Blue Dragon Console and analyze the disks.

Egypt

The train ride to Egypt is interesting and action-packed, to say the least. However, the enemies aboard this ultra-modern conveyance must have gotten their battle training at Dweebs R Us. If you can't defeat the train's guards, you'd better sell your Nintendo Entertainment System and use the money for physical therapy.

On the other hand, getting over the pyramid takes practice. As you're going down the opposite side, jump over the rock generators. Perfect this maneuver, and the generators won't have a chance to shoot, let alone do damage.

Inside the pyramid, head toward the top, where you'll find a vertical passage that you can scale only with the difficult triangle jump. Practice doesn't seem to help with this one. The timing required is, I believe, beyond the abilities of most mortals. The only trick is to keep trying. You want the water boots, don't you?

If you think the first triangle jump should be banned by the SPCNM (Society for the Prevention of Cruelty to Nintendo Masters), wait until you get to the second one, just after the water area. Accomplishing this second triangle jump is the only way back to the surface. It's also the only way to get key 2.

Kazakh Again

Now that you have key 2, you can access the S-2 corridor, at the top of Kazakh base. To get there, follow the route to S-1, except go one level higher.

In the S-2 corridor, you'll battle a guard on a one-wheeled motorcycle. Blast the motorcycle as it comes toward you, then jump to let it pass beneath. About six hits puts this wheeled demon out of commission.

After defeating the motorcycle guard, continue left down the corridor. Beyond the next door . . . why, it's your friend Kain! Rescue him, and you'll receive file 3.

Japan

Upon analyzing file 3, you'll discover that your mission involves more than rescuing Kain. A secret project, partly run by Strider itself, must be stopped. You can find more evidence in Japan, so why are you standing around in Kazakh? Get moving!

The Japanese base is small. You should have your Plasma Arrow and file 4 in no time.

China

The Chinese base is divided into two sections. You'll come here twice, but on this trip bypass the first transporter, jump off the top of the base, and fall to the right. At the bottom you'll see the second half of the base on the right. Enter and work your way up to the top, where you'll find the magnetic boots and get a helpful message from a secret friend.

Kazakh Yet Again

Remember the strange glowing floor you found at the end of the S-1 corridor? (If you don't remember the glowing floor, you probably didn't follow the corridor all the way to the end the first time you were in it.) Now that you have the magnetic boots, not only can you cross that floor, but you can also walk up the wall on the far left and across the ceiling as well. In a secret room, high above the rest of the base, look for key 4.

Back to China

Key 4 opens the left half of the Chinese base. This part of the base is unlike the section where you found the magnetic boots. It's large, complicated, and filled with dangerous traps and enemies.

First, work your way down until you come to an area with moving platforms. You have a choice here. You can ride the platforms to the left, or you can drop down the shaft on the right. The right-hand path leads to the attack boots, which give you the power to slide into enemies, using your feet as a weapon. I suggest going this way first. Once you have the boots, take the transporter to the top, re-enter the base, and make your way back down.

This time, take the moving platforms to the left. After a ride up an elevator and a drop down a long shaft filled with spiked wheels, you'll come to a room containing strange machinery and a huge statue. A square object, which shoots deadly white pellets, circles the room. As the square moves toward you, blast it, jumping to let it pass beneath you. After jumping, run behind the square and keep shooting.

When you destroy the square, the statue will start shooting. Blast its center a few times, and you'll get key 3.

Another Trip to Kazakh

Key 3 opens the last section of Kazakh, a long and winding corridor loaded with spiked floors, rock generators, wrong turns, and vicious enemies. At the end of this corridor is another statue room. This time the circling square moves faster. You need to jump just right in order to shoot and still get out of its path. Your plasma arrow helps here. In addition, keep close watch on your life energy. If it gets too low, restore it with the medical power trick.

When you destroy this statue, file 5 will drop into your grimy little hands. Hooray!

Africa

You'll find file 6 in the African base, but not before successfully navigating the jungle and infiltrating the base's icy corridors, tasks that require practice. Inside the base, you need exceptional jumping skills. Feats of derring-do include bounding over a series of nests (which fall when touched) and jumping from one moving platform to another in order to cross a large chasm.

Unfortunately, when it comes to jumping, *Strider* is not exactly responsive to the control pad, making the obstacles here even tougher. Patience.

Get past that chasm? Then you must have found another statue room. Get rid of the circling square and the statue; then collect file 6.

Los Angeles

File 6 leads to the city of the angels—exciting Los Angeles. The base here is no match for a skillful soldier like you. Remember one thing: Not everything you hear is true. When an enemy says something can't be done, don't believe him. Do it anyway and collect key 5.

Australia

Before you reach the entrance to the Australian base you'll need to make a long, difficult jump over spike-covered ground. Before trying the last jump, stand as close to the edge of the pedestal as you can. This will give you the best chance of success. If you fall into the spikes, it's almost impossible to get out.

Strangely enough, the Australian base connects with the African base. If you don't get lost, this second African trek won't be as trying as the first. Work your way down, until you find the last statue room. If you wind up in familiar territory, you took a wrong turn.

Red Dragon Base

After destroying the last statue in Australia, travel to the Red Dragon Base, where you must destroy two computer systems and face Matic in a deadly duel. The Red Dragon Base is large and confusing; prepare to take some wrong turns. In addition, getting past some areas requires top-notch jumping skills. Remember to use the acceleration jump whenever it can help. (If you don't know what an acceleration jump is, read your manual.)

The Red Dragon Base is, of course, crawling with boss soldiers. Some you've seen before; others you haven't. One new boss is Flash Blade, a savage fighter until you learn his Achilles' heel—blast him when he's in the air. That'll set him into a crazy spin. While he's spinning, avoid him. When he stops, zap him into another spin. It'll take a few shots to defeat him.

One door in the base can be opened only after you've destroyed the two master computers. The first computer is near the top of the building. Go up until you see a room whose floor is made of many transporters. To get to the second computer, climb the outside wall of the base, using your magnetic boots.

After you destroy both computers, go back to the locked door (it'll open now). Here you'll fight several more boss soldiers and, finally, Matic himself.

May your Strider training serve you well!

Metal Gear

Company: *Ultra*
Type: *Military Adventure*

The Game

Objective: Infiltrate the Outer Heaven base, rescue Dr. Petrowitch and his daughter, and destroy Metal Gear.

Organization: The game is divided into *rooms* that connect to form the buildings and outside scenes of the Outer Heaven base. Unlike many games of this type, this game has no scrolling areas. Rather, the entire screen changes as you move from room to room.

Creatures: Because this is a military game, most of your enemies are soldiers like you. However, boss soldiers, including Machine Gun Kid, Bulltank, Coward Duck, and Fire Trooper, possess powerful weapons and specialized skills.

General Strategy: This is an infiltration mission. Advance as far as you can without being seen. Search everywhere. You must locate many objects, most of which are required to complete the game.

The Controls

Move left, right, forward, or back.
Select items on weapons and equipment screens.
When using a transceiver, press ← or → to change frequency, ↑ to send message.
Select command from command window.

Fire weapon.
Choose certain items from equipment screen.
Finalize selection of command from command window.

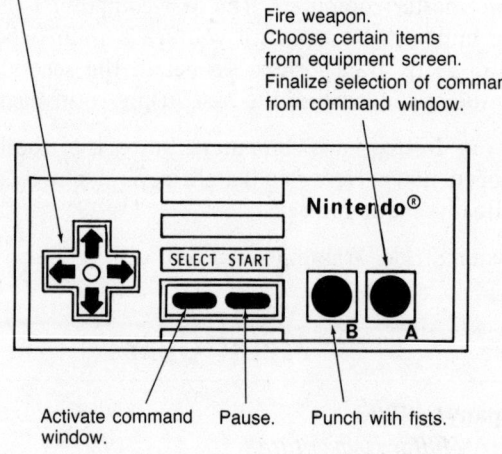

Activate command window.   Pause.   Punch with fists.

The Challenge

There's something special about *Metal Gear*, although I've never determined exactly what. I do know it's got something to do with the game's strategy. How many video games encourage you to avoid the enemy, to remain, whenever possible, unseen? Don't get me wrong, *Metal Gear*'s not all stealth and hiding. You can bet that your control pad will get a workout. But you'll have to try a different strategy than usual.

Strategies

Think infiltration—avoid fights whenever you can. This isn't *Friday the 13th, Part 12: Jason Takes Outer Heaven*. A high body count won't impress anyone (except maybe Jason and his colleague Freddy Kruger).

Make a map so you'll know the quickest route to each location. Yes, I know *Metal Gear* comes with a complete map, but take a word of advice—don't use it. The map gives away too much of the game. You want to get your money's worth, don't you?

As you rescue prisoners, your rank increases. Kill a prisoner, and your rank decreases. Don't laugh! It's easy to accidentally shoot and kill a prisoner. So when prisoners speak, use the arrow pad to advance the text, not the fire button.

Keep the enemy at a distance. When a guard gets close, he can kill you almost instantly.

Many supplies are available in unlimited quantities. (Unfortunately, the quantity you can carry *is* limited.) When you find rations, for example, you can stock up by grabbing the canister then exiting and re-entering the room. Another canister of rations replaces the one you took.

Finally, some doors in the base are invisible. When you're stuck without an exit, or when you can't locate an object, pound on walls. A special glove, which you'll find later in the game, will help you locate these sneaky entrances and exits.

Area 1

Phase one of your mission is to get into the base. Slip past the guards and their dogs, fighting only when necessary, then stow away in the truck that will take you deep into Outer Heaven. At first, the beginning of the game may seem difficult. But it's as easy as squashing ants once you master a few tricks. For example, if you learn their attack pattern, the guard dogs won't have a chance. Run fast, though. To these ferocious beasts you look like a giant can of Alpo.

Some guards are ready for action. Others are sound asleep. Deal with the alert guards by sneaking up while their backs are turned.

Check every truck. Handy equipment may be stashed anywhere. You can't afford to pass it up.

Building 1

Begin your investigation with Building 1. The door is locked, you say? Of course it is. You didn't think you'd walk right in and take over, did you? If you followed my advice and examined every vehicle you passed, you found Card 1, a magnetic key. If you don't have Card 1, go back and find it.

Building 1 has three floors and a roof. (Yes, I know most buildings have roofs. This one's different. You'll find rooms up there.) First, explore the building, examining every room you can. For now, you can enter only those rooms which respond to Card 1. Be patient and check everywhere. Find the gas mask and the hand gun.

Your first prisoners are on the second floor. There are also some treacherous traps. Watch your step.

Some rooms are monitored by cameras. As with the guards, don't let the cameras see you.

Some rooms in Building 1 contain goodies like electrified floors or poison gas. Deadly stuff. Eventually, you'll have the equipment to thwart any obstacle. If something seems impossible now, be patient. The solution will present itself.

Items in Building 1 include the hand gun, the gas mask, the machine gun, remote-control missiles, the infrared goggles, the iron glove, the mine detector, and the silencer. In addition, you'll run across some prisoners and meet two boss soldiers—Machine Gun Kid and Twin Shot. You can kill Machine Gun Kid with just about any weapon; however, you might find that the remote-control missiles work best. Grenades work well on the Twin Shots.

You'll come back to Building 1 several times before your mission is complete.

Area 2

To get to area 2, stow away in a truck. You figure out which one. On your map, note which truck goes where. You'll thank yourself later.

Area 2's most interesting features are its mine fields and the big tank guarding the entrance to building 2. The maze through which you must travel to building 4 is a treat, too. Luckily, it isn't overly difficult to solve. Also in this area, you'll find the back door to building 1 and three new trucks to explore.

Two puzzling problems—how to defeat the tank and how to enter building 2. You can take out the tank with only one type of weapon—and lots of it. If you can't enter building 2, maybe you should disguise yourself.

Building 2

Here, you'll find some nasty obstacles, notably the deep, water-filled gutters. You can walk through some areas of the gutters, although you'll sink up to your waist. The deep areas require special equipment.

Items in building 2 include the antenna, Card 5, Card 6, Card 7, Card 8, the rocket launcher, the compass, and the antidote. You'll also have to face Bulltank, Coward Duck, and the Arnolds (three more boss soldiers). The rocket launcher works best with the Arnolds. Use grenades on Bulltank. Any weapon will upset Coward Duck.

Area 3

This area is accessible from the back door of building 2. Its most notable features are the desert, a maze (yep, another one), and the entrances to buildings 3 and 5. Once again, the maze is not overly difficult to solve. Crossing the desert, on the other hand, requires two important items—something to heal scorpion bites and something to help you find your way.

Building 3

Building 3 is small. In fact, until the end of the game, only a couple of rooms here will interest you, one of which contains an important item.

After you've rescued Dr. Petrowitch and his daughter, come back to Building 3 for your final confrontation. The Super Computer is located here, as is your ultimate adversary. I won't say who he is. You'll be surprised.

If you have trouble destroying the Super Computer, you're probably not using the right weapon. Only one type will work, and you need a slew of it. (Hint: it's not something you shoot.)

Building 4

Access building 4 from area 2. This building is loaded with pitfalls, so watch your step. Moreover, the pitfall areas are dark. You can fix that problem, if you find the right item.

Items you'll find here include the bomb blast suit, Card 3, and Dr. Petrowitch's daughter, what an item! There's a boss soldier here, too—Shotgunner. He's a piece of cake to beat, as long as you still have your weapons. (Yes, I have a reason for saying that, as you'll discover when you play.)

Building 5

This building is comprised of only six rooms. Somewhere here are three secret doors. Pound the walls.

Also, find the flashlight and Dr. Petrowitch. The good doctor is guarded by Fire Trooper, one of the boss soldiers. Fire Trooper is so easy to beat that I'm not going to give you any hints. If you're stumped, turn in your Nintendo Master Gamer ID card.

Secret! Secret!

If you can't locate the compass and the rocket launcher, read the following paragraph.

Obtaining the compass and the rocket launcher is tricky. They are in building 2, but you can get them only if you have reached a four-star rank and have called Jennifer on frequency 12048 before entering the room. Which room? You figure it out.

Defender of the Crown

Company: *Ultra*
Type: *Strategy War Game*

The Game

Objective: To capture all the Norman castles and claim the kingship for the Saxons.

Organization: Most of the game is played on a map of England that's divided into territories. You must move your army into a territory in order to claim it. The game also includes arcade scenes in which you participate in a tournament, lay siege to a castle, raid a castle, or rescue a damsel in distress.

Creatures: No creatures here. This is a serious game of conquest in medieval England. Your opponents are Norman soldiers and knights, and occasional disloyal Saxons.

General Strategy: Conquer new territories to build up your army. The more territory you own, the higher your income. Soldiers and battle equipment are expensive, even in the middle ages. Of course, to conquer new territory you must have a strong army—or at least a stronger army than your opponent's. Sound like a vicious circle? It is!

The Controls

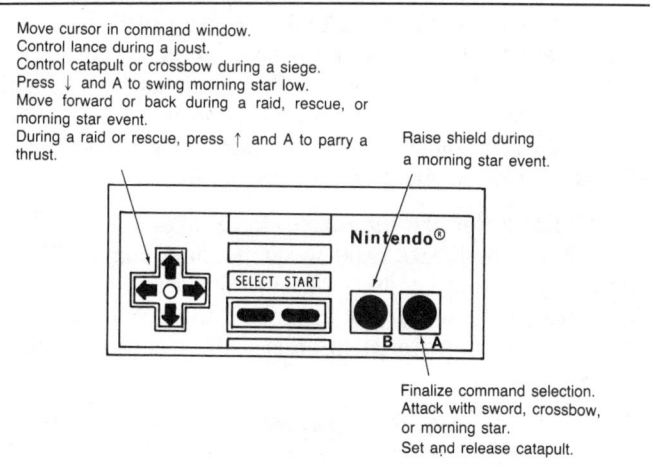

Move cursor in command window.
Control lance during a joust.
Control catapult or crossbow during a siege.
Press ↓ and A to swing morning star low.
Move forward or back during a raid, rescue, or morning star event.
During a raid or rescue, press ↑ and A to parry a thrust.

Raise shield during a morning star event.

Finalize command selection.
Attack with sword, crossbow, or morning star.
Set and release catapult.

The Challenge

Defender of the Crown is a challenging game, one that takes a while to master. If you're easily frustrated, this game may not be for you. But if you're a fan of war games and like the idea of a little arcade action thrown in to break the monotony, *Defender of the Crown* belongs on your shelf.

Strategies

This is a game of high finance as much as a game of strategy and power. Why? As our national debt proves, building an army is expensive. What with catapults going for 15 gold pieces and castles for an incredible 20, a Saxon lord has no choice but to spread his influence as far as he can, gaining new territories and building a bigger tax base. Conquering new territory, then, is the name of the game. Not only does it give you a tidy income with which to build your forces, but it also weakens your enemies by limiting their expansion.

In the beginning of the game, much of Britain is unclaimed. Winning new territory is as simple as moving a single soldier onto the area you want. Unfortunately, it's rare that you can conquer more than two extra territories this way. After all, your enemies (and allies) have plans too.

Once all territories on the map are claimed, you can expand your influence by taking territories from other lords. This means fighting, so you'll need a strong army. Return to your castle and start buying solders, knights, and catapults. When you're building your army, keep in mind that although you need many soldiers to defend your castle, the knights and catapults give you the greatest strength in the field.

When a Norman (or Saxon!) force takes over one of your territories, get it back. And waste no time doing it! If your army is too weak to drive out the invaders, get help from Robin Hood. (You can do this three times per game.) You *must* keep your territories in order to have enough money for a good-sized army.

Once you've got a respectable army, you can take them into the field. But don't forget to leave plenty of soldiers behind—at least 30—to defend the homestead.

How strong an army is required to successfully attack an occupied territory? That depends on the size of your opponent's army, which, unfortunately, is something you have no way of knowing. One thing you can count on—the Norman forces grow faster than yours. In fact, I suspect that *Defender of the Crown* cheats. In the time it takes you to build an army of, say, 37 soldiers and 2 knights, the Norman forces may have been built up to something like 43 soldiers and 12 knights.

Where do they get the cash to buy such a large army? Beats me. Maybe they rob little old ladies in their spare time.

In any case, you should consider attacking only when you have at least 6 knights, one catapult, and maybe 20 soldiers. Then hope that the territory you invade is not guarded by a large force like the one mentioned above.

Whatever you do, no matter how bad things get, never, *never* retreat from a battle. Retreating makes your lord look like a jerk, and you lose leadership points, which give you an advantage in battle. These points are too important to squander. Better to take a few lumps than look like a coward.

You can increase your leadership points in a couple of ways. Rescue a princess, which is good for your hero status, not to mention your social life, or attend a tournament.

The Battleground

Attacking an occupied territory has either of two results. If you have an extremely strong army, your opponent may surrender the territory without a fight. Otherwise, you'll be brought to the combat screen.

On the combat screen you can choose from among several battle tactics—ferocious attack, hold your ground, bombard, outflank, or retreat. The manual gives hints as to when to use these different tactics, although in actual play the differences between them seem slight. Unless you have a larger army than your opponent, you will almost certainly lose the fight. In general, the following tactics seems to work best:

- ❏ Never retreat. Losing leadership is not worth saving a few men's lives. (Undoubtedly, the men, if they could speak, would express a different opinion, eh?)
- ❏ If you have catapults, use Bombard.
- ❏ If you have a strong army, particularly one with many knights, a ferocious attack seems to work well. (The manual suggests this is a risky tactic that may work best for weak leaders with small armies—in other words, for lords who have nothing to lose. Try it both ways and see what works best for you.)
- ❏ In most cases hold your ground. This is more or less the straight attack tactic—no tricks, no special equipment, just simple hand-to-hand combat.

No matter what tactic you choose, the computer (yes, your NES is actually a computer) has an advantage. Don't you hate cheaters?

The Tournament

Any lord—even you—can hold a tournament. If you host one, it'll cost you five gold pieces to pay the expenses. If one of the other lords holds a tournament, you will be expected to attend. Free admission.

By the time a tournament is called, you should have used the "Read Map" command to learn which lords are the weakest jousters. Then, when you're asked to choose an opponent, pick the wimp. Weak jousters include Geoffrey, Edmund, and Cedric.

A tournament consists of two events—the joust and the morning star. The winner of the joust enters the morning star event with additional strength, so winning the first contest gives you a strong advantage. However, if you lose the joust, it's still possible to win with the morning star. It's this event that determines the tournament's champion.

There is little to say about these events. The manual that came with your game adequately describes all you need to know. However, for those who would like a brief review, here are the basics:

❏ In the joust event, aim your lance at the center of your opponent's shield. Whatever you do, don't accidentally (or deliberately) spear your opponent's horse. If you do, you will be disgraced and lose most of your possessions.

❏ In the morning star event, learn to use your shield effectively. (At the very least, keep the shield up by holding button B as you fight.) Press button A to attack when your morning star is furthest from your opponent. This yields the strongest swing. It takes practice to master the timing.

If you win three consecutive morning star events, you'll be proclaimed tournament champion, which is wonderful for your leadership rating.

A final tournament hint: Before a joust begins, you must decide whether to compete for fame or land. Never compete for land unless you're confident you can win. Land represents income. You can't afford to lose it.

The Raid

There's more than one way to earn extra cash. If you're feeling cocky, you may want to raid another lord's castle and steal his gold. A raid is tough to pull off, though. As one of my consultants said, *Defender of the Crown* must come with a GLS chip —Good Luck Sucker.

At the beginning of a raid, three guards will try to defend the castle. Beating them is easy, since you have about a five-to-one advantage. However, you'll meet a fourth swordsman who's much stronger than the first three. The computer almost always wins.

Fortunately, you can win *Defender of the Crown* without resorting to raids. Although it's tempting to steal cash, you'll soon find that the odds are stacked against you.

If there's something I've missed, if you know the trick to a successful raid (assuming there is a trick), let me know.

The Siege

Whenever you attack an opponent's castle, you must conduct a siege. This requires at least one catapult. Using a catapult is easy once you get the hang of it. The trick is to know how far back to pull the catapult before releasing it—the farther back, the higher the shot.

Your catapult comes with three types of ammunition— boulders, disease, and greek fire. In order to achieve the best effect, use the ammunition like this:

1. Destroy the top of the wall with a boulder. Do this first because, until you've breached the wall, nothing can penetrate the castle.
2. Follow the boulder with disease, firing it with the same pull used on the boulder. When employed early in a siege, disease has time to infect most of the enemy soldiers.
3. Next, launch the greek fire. Each successful shot will kill 10% of the castle's guards.
4. Finally, continue with boulders, demolishing the wall piece by piece. Pull back the catapult less and less in order to shoot lower and lower. Watch the number of

men remaining in the castle, and cease fire if the count drops to zero.

If you don't take over the castle or garrison in the catapult phase of the siege, the surviving occupants will attack. You'll then enter the hand-to-hand combat phase. All the rules of combat mentioned above apply.

Besieged

Just as you can lay siege to an enemy castle (or garrison), so too can an enemy lay siege to yours. When this happens, expect a fierce fight. Use your crossbow to kill the enemy soldiers as they come over the wall. The enemy soldiers are formidable archers. Each time they fire, your strength line drops one notch.

Your best defense against a siege is to maintain a large force in your castle. If you're caught with an inadequate army, hang it up.

Damsels in Distress

No medieval scenario would be complete without a kidnapped lady or two. *Defender of the Crown* is no exception. Since the daughter of a lord can command a high ransom, an occasional abduction is to be expected.

So, if an ally asks you to rescue his daughter, accept. A refusal will brand you a coward and lower your leadership rating. However, if you accept the quest and you fail, your leadership rating will suffer anyway. Yep. It's the old rock and a hard place. Since you can't refuse gracefully, you may as well accept. Makes your decision easier, don't you think?

Handle a rescue the same way you would a raid. If you succeed, you'll not only increase your leadership rating (everyone likes a hero), but you'll also be granted the lady's hand in marriage.

What's that? You're a confirmed bachelor? Too bad. Marry her anyway. You're a bachelorette? Well, you shouldn't have disguised yourself as an English lord. Shame on you!

Final Words

As in many war games, the outcome of battles is determined by the roll of the die, so to speak. All you can do is give yourself the best chance and toss your fate to the computer's random number generator. In this case, the odds are stacked against you.

Nevertheless, it is possible not only to win but to win often. It's just a matter of dealing with the game's eccentricities (and dishonest gameplay) and working within the restrictions forced upon you.

Keep practicing. After all, if you win, you'll discover who stole the king's crown.

And before you even ask, the answer is no. I won't tell you who has the crown. I promised Robin I'd keep it a secret.

ARCADE

Arcade

Super Mario Bros. 3

Company: *Nintendo*
Type: *Arcade Jump-Run-Shoot Contest*

The Game

Objective: To save the princess and the Mushroom World by defeating Bowser and his seven Koopa kids.

Organization: The Mushroom World is broken down into eight kingdoms, each of which is divided into several scrolling levels. Extra areas include fortresses, ships, and other locations.

Creatures: *Super Mario Bros. 3* is filled with monsters from Mario games of the past, including Koopa Troopa, the Hammer Brothers, and Goombas. In addition, you'll face new enemies like the Chain Chomp, Dry Bones, and Walking Piranhas.

General Strategy: Unlike most NES games, you must read the manual in order to beat *Super Mario Bros. 3*. Otherwise, you'll miss much of what the game offers. *Super Mario Bros. 3* is bursting with bonus items, such as mushrooms, which make Mario big; leaves, which give Mario a tail for attacking or flying; and frog suits, which allow Mario to swim faster. In addition, there are the usual coins and 1-ups. Always be on the look-out for bonus items. Sometimes they're deviously hidden.

The Controls

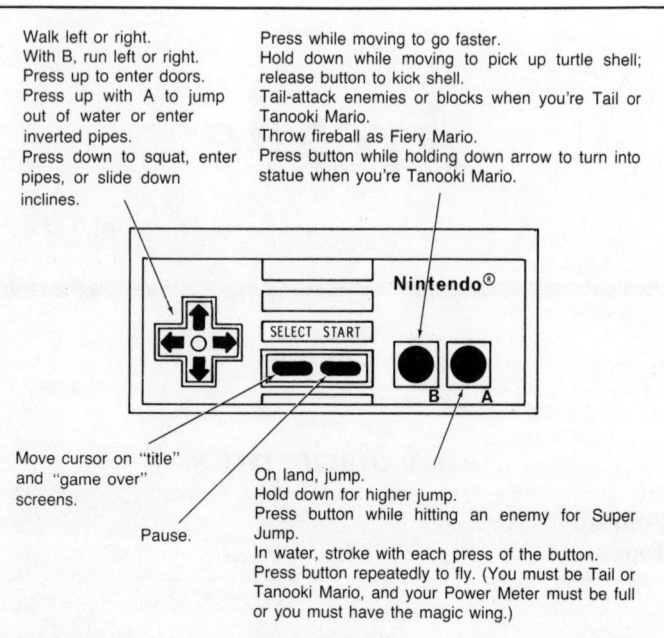

Walk left or right.
With B, run left or right.
Press up to enter doors.
Press up with A to jump out of water or enter inverted pipes.
Press down to squat, enter pipes, or slide down inclines.

Press while moving to go faster.
Hold down while moving to pick up turtle shell; release button to kick shell.
Tail-attack enemies or blocks when you're Tail or Tanooki Mario.
Throw fireball as Fiery Mario.
Press button while holding down arrow to turn into statue when you're Tanooki Mario.

Move cursor on "title" and "game over" screens.

Pause.

On land, jump.
Hold down for higher jump.
Press button while hitting an enemy for Super Jump.
In water, stroke with each press of the button.
Press button repeatedly to fly. (You must be Tail or Tanooki Mario, and your Power Meter must be full or you must have the magic wing.)

The Challenge

Super Mario Bros. 3 is a huge game. If we tried to cover it level by level, we'd have to give it a book of its own! For this reason, instead of detailed descriptions of each world, we'll look at the game in a general way, giving hints, strategies, and special techniques that will help you in any level. Following that, we'll tell you about some special stuff to look for.

Strategies

Getting a mushroom can be difficult, since you can't always tell from which direction it'll exit the block. Jump on top of the block as the mushroom surfaces, and you'll rarely miss your target.

You must map some areas of the game. In the later stages, you need to know where certain tubes and doors will take you.

As with other Super Mario games, hit every block, even those without question marks.

If you can find no exit, jump around a bit. Hidden items and bonuses are everywhere, even off the screen. In open areas, fly over the terrain in search of bonuses.

Some bonuses are hidden in blocks. To get them, smack the block with your tail (if you are Tail Mario) or with a turtle shell.

One special item, the switch box, will change blocks into coins, and vice versa. Why would you want to change coins into blocks? Coins are nice, but sometimes it's more important to have stepping stones.

Try to enter every tube. Some contain bonus areas, coins, special items, and shortcuts.

When you reach the end of an area, you must grab a card. To have the best chance of getting a star card, stand back a ways, then run while holding button B and jump in an arc towards the card. Gather three stars, and you'll get a 5-up!

There are only eight different layouts of the N-Mark Spade Panels. Keep track of them. You'll be able to build your supply of coins, items, and reserve Marios easily.

Watch your item inventory. If you exceed 28 items, the last item you received will be replaced by the new item.

When in the forced-scrolling worlds, such as World 1-4, stay toward the right side of the screen. You will have more time to maneuver and to break blocks as you look for special items.

To get past a block tosser, get up close when it attacks; the block it throws will then arc over your head. When the coast is clear, jump on him.

To destroy the Koopa in each world's fortress, jump on him three times. After each jump, move away, because when he springs back up, he'll try to pounce on you. When he does, quickly leap onto his back again.

Did you know that you can get 1-ups by jumping on enemies? It's true. Just leap-frog across the backs of nine enemies, without touching the ground, and you'll earn a single 1-up. Nobody said it was easy!

When you're a Tail Mario, double your points by swinging your tail the instant you land on an enemy's back.

If you want to stay safe from a cannon and still score points, stand on top of the cannon just in front of the mouth. When the cannonball appears, it'll hit your feet, racking up points just as if you had jumped on it.

When you find the big green boot in World 5, enter the boot and stomp everything you meet.

Specific Hints

Early in World 1-1, you'll see three coins that angle up into the sky. They lead to your first chance to fly and to a block containing a 1-up.

At the first set of gold blocks in World 1-3, jump on the right-hand turtle and bounce him left, into the middle of the blocks. Then jump in the open area between the blocks until you find a red musical-note block. Leap from this block to get to a bonus world loaded with coins. (If you're a Tail Mario, fly over the fourth set of coins for a 1-up mushroom.)

World 1-5 has a bonus area, too. At the first opening to the overground, there's a musical-note block on the left side of the exit. Use it to leap up into the sky. Again, if you're a Tail Mario, fly over the fourth set of coins to get a 1-up. There are many other red musical-note blocks in the game. Find them all!

Have you ever found a magic whistle? These wonderful items let you warp to higher levels, so they're important if you want to beat the game. To get the whistle in World 1-3, stand in the center of the long white block near the end of the level. Kill the turtle. Now hold down on the controller until you drop behind the scenery. Head to the right. See the treasure chest? It holds the whistle.

The mini-fortress of World 1 contains another magic whistle, but you must be a Tail Mario to get it. Here's how: After the lava, stomp on Dry Bones, then head toward the door. Don't exit yet. Instead, accelerate left, and fly up after hitting the single block that's over the lava. (Don't hit your head on the Rotodisc.) Fly up and to the right. You'll fly out of the picture, but the screen will stop scrolling when you hit the end. At this point, push up on the controller. You'll drop into the room that contains the second whistle.

World 2-3 has tons of coins, although some are tricky to get. At the second pyramid of small blocks, jump straight up from the block to the left of the peak. You'll find a musical-note block. Use it as a step to find more blocks above. In the sky are coins and a set of blocks. One block contains a switch box. Grab it to change blocks into coins. Return to the ground. The left pyramid is now a stack of coins, with a 1-up mushroom.

Did you find the vine in World 2-5? No? Near the end of the level is a small corridor filled with gold blocks. Throw a turtle shell into it.

World 3-1 contains a secret question-mark box. After the underwater area, press yourself against the left edge of the blocks. Push up and hit button A. You'll leap right out of the picture. Move Mario to the left and find a small water-filled room.

If you're a Tail Mario when you get to the end of World 3-2, you can find a 1-up mushroom above the card.

In World 3-3, in order to avoid traveling a long way underwater, find the switch box and change coins into a bridge.

World 3-7 has a bonus area. To find it, go to where a turtle is closed in by blocks on a double-decker platform. Kick the turtle to reveal a vine. Climb the vine up to the clouds. Wow! Look at the coins! There's another bonus area to the right of the vine. To find it, jump in the middle of the cloud platform. You'll find a musical-note block. Bounce on the block and find a chest.

Need more Marios? In World 3-9 take a turtle shell past the white panel and throw it between the two cannons. Move to the platform above, so that both cannons are visible. The turtle shell will now take care of the cannon balls, racking up free lives for you.

If you're a Tail Mario when you enter World 4, fly up at the beginning of the level and find a bonus room with two 1-ups. Watch out for the fish.

In the second mini-fortress of World 4, if you get the switch block, a square of coins and a secret door will appear.

The door leads to a bonus area. Search for four 1-up mushrooms.

At the beginning of World 5-1, there is a tube above you. You can get to it easily if you use the magic wing. If you don't have the magic wing, there's another way—but it's only for the best Nintendo Master. If you think you're ready, read on.

(We're going to assume you're a mini-Mario at this point.) Enter the level, then dodge the little beetle that comes toward you. Retrieve the mushroom in the wooden block, without getting hit by the first Chain Chomp. Now here's the hard part: Get to the right of the second Chain Chomp by leaping toward his anchor block as he is stretching. Then jump past him. (This technique won't work if he clobbers you; you'll have to try again with your next Mario.) Now, grab the leaf in the question-mark block. Climb up on the block, and blast out through the top. Return to the beginning—watch those Chain Chomps—and clear the gold blocks so you have some open space.

Next, move right, getting as close to the first Chain Chomp as you safely can and run to the left, watching your power meter. If you've done it right, you can move fast enough to get your Tail Mario to fly. At this point, fly up and enter the tube over the beginning of the level. You'll enter an ice room with an exit tube on the bottom right. (There's a treasure chest past the thin corridor on the right; you need the magic wing to get it.) Exit through the tube, and you'll pass under this level's blocks.

There are a couple of things to do here. First, one by one, get the 1-ups in the blocks to the right of the exit tube. (If you try to get them all at once, they'll cancel each other out.) Then build up speed, fly straight up, and hit the left block in the trio. A switch block will appear. Use it to grab some coins. Need some extra Marios? Let the timer run out. Then repeat the moves.

In World 6, slide on the ice while crouching to get under obstacles. Also, in the first mini-fortress, change into a statue in order to protect yourself from the moving flames.

To get rid of Spike in World 6-6, lure him toward you by dropping down to his level. When he gets close, jump back up above him, then step down on his head.

Even if you're a Tail Mario on World 6-9, you can fly only with the magic wing. And speaking of World 6-9, did you find the gold switch block near the end? It changes enemies into coins. Don't get cocky—it's only a short-term transformation.

The World 6 Koopa is hard to beat. Use the ball, and time your jumps carefully.

In World 7-2, there's a hidden bridge of musical-note blocks. Find all the blocks. Then use the tube to get onto the bridge.

Getting low on Marios? In the first mini-fortress, enter the room that's filled with gold blocks, go under the ledge in the center, and find the switch block. Jump on it. The room will glitter with coins. Get as many coins as you can before they change back. Now what? Exit, re-enter, and repeat the process. You can get up to 99 Marios. Really!

Clear out the bomb soldiers in World 8 before they can overwhelm you. To get out of the line of fire, jump up onto the cannons. Also, destroy all the Rocky Wrenches. If you don't, you may get caught in lethal cross-fire.

At the beginning of World 8-1, fly into the sky and find a bonus area.

At the beginning of World 8-2, jump into the sand slide for a shortcut. If you want a leaf, enter the tube on the left. If you want coins, enter the tube on the right.

In the Castle of Koopa, accelerate to full speed in order to zip past the three laser-firing statues. When you reach the top of the stairs, jump over to the right-hand ledge and leap up. Now you can grab a 1-up mushroom.

The last enemy you must battle is a giant Koopa. Believe it or not, he's easy to beat. As the Koopa jumps, stay directly under him. Each time he hits the ground, he'll break some blocks. When there's only one row of blocks left, move out of his way, and he'll fall through the floor. Now enter the colored door and rescue the princess. (She'll play a nasty joke on you.)

Game over!

Mega Man 2

Company: *Capcom*
Type: *Arcade Action*

The Game

Objective: To conquer the eight worlds of Dr. Wily's boss creations, then take on Skull Castle—Dr. Wily's hideaway.

Organization: The worlds in *Mega Man 2* are constructed of vertically or horizontally scrolling scenes. Your last objective, Skull Castle, is the greatest challenge, with more than six different areas of sizzling action.

Creatures: The most significant creatures are the level bosses: Bubble Man, Air Man, Quick Man, Heat Man, Wood Man, Metal Man, Flash Man, and Crash Man. You'll also meet many other less-powerful enemies, such as walkers, lobsters, bats, hot dogs, lightning lords, gear clowns, and prop-tops.

General Strategy: Because you can complete the initial eight levels in any order, learn which boss has the best weapon for the next level you'll be playing. (Remember, when you defeat a boss, you get his weapon.) The ideal order in which to play the levels is not the order in which they appear on the selection screen.

The Controls

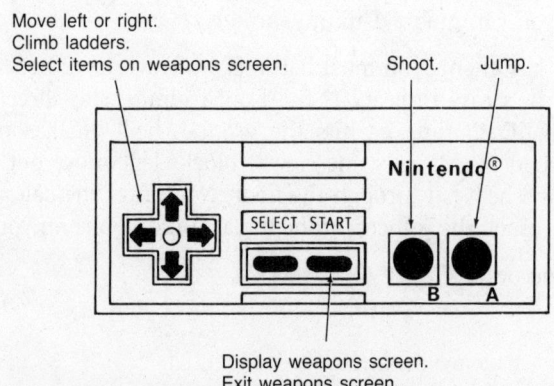

Move left or right.
Climb ladders.
Select items on weapons screen.

Shoot.

Jump.

Display weapons screen.
Exit weapons screen.

The Challenge

Mega Man 2 is a challenging game, but with practice, you'll advance steadily toward your final conflict with Dr. Wily. Because this is a fairly short game, it's unlikely you'll grow bored before you locate Dr. Wily, and you have a good chance of getting to the end.

Got your dancing shoes on? Then let's go!

Strategies

Most creatures in *Mega Man 2* are easy to beat . . . if you study their movements. For example, the flying fish can get annoying with their egg droppings. However, once you learn when they're going to release their cargo, you can start blasting eggs like a pro.

Sometimes defeated enemies leave behind life-energy and weapon-energy capsules. These capsules appear so often that you have no excuse for dying in battle. The only excusable deaths for Mega Man are those caused by falling or by touching something like underwater mines.

The "E" capsule, which allows you to refill your energies at any time, is another special item to watch for. When you find one, carry it with you until you need it. You can even use it when fighting a boss. Unlike the life-energy and weapon-energy capsules, the "E" capsules are not dropped by defeated enemies. Rather, they are hidden throughout Dr. Wily's strange world. When you find one, don't waste it. Use it only as a last resort. The "E" capsules can make the difference between winning and losing. In fact, some obstacles are almost impossible to overcome without them.

When you defeat certain levels, you're awarded one of three valuable devices—the levitation platform, the jet sled, and the elevator platform. Like the weapons you obtain from the bosses, these devices are most helpful in specific levels. You'll need these devices to obtain some other important items.

Now let's take a detailed look at the worlds of *Mega Man 2.*

Air Man

Air Man's world is the easiest to beat. That's not to say you won't have to put out some effort. After all, you didn't lay down fifty green ones for a punchout with Pee Wee Herman. The air tikis, for example, are sure to have you banging your head against a wall and snapping at loved ones. To get passed an air tiki, wait for its horns to descend. Then high-tail it across its head and onto the next platform. Once on the platform, destroy any air gremlins that attack, and then continue over the next air tiki.

Air tikis are like a drive past the beach on bikini day, compared with lightning lords. You must hijack each of the lightning lords' clouds, one after the other, until you reach the next platform. The timing is tricky. While riding one cloud, blast the lightning lord from the next. Sometimes you must jump into thin air, trusting that the cloud will drift up under you before you fall.

Flying fish abound in this level. Blast their eggs before they hit the ground. If the eggs burst, you'll have to contend with a flurry of deadly feathers. (Deadly feathers? On fish??)

Air Man's weapon is a tornado, which he produces with the spinning blades in his belly. Get close, jumping over the tornadoes whenever you can, then blast him.

Bubble Man

Falling, which costs you one life, is the biggest danger in this level. Jump carefully, especially when crossing platforms that drop out from under you. You can stand on them for only a split second.

After your jumping ordeal, enter the underwater caverns, where you'll take on the huge lantern fish. They aren't as tough as they look. Shoot for the lights on top of their heads.

The ceilings and walls of Bubble Man's world are covered with deadly spiked mines. As luck would have it, Mega Man has to do some serious jumping in this world. Those mines are right overhead, a constant threat. Remember that the longer you hold button A, the higher you jump. Learn to control the height of your jumps, and you'll never lose a life to the mines.

Finally, you'll fight an underwater battle with Bubble Man himself. He attacks with bubble lead. When released, these heavy bubbles fall to the ground and roll toward you. As you fight, jump over the bubbles, blasting Bubble Man whenever you've got a clear shot.

Crash Man

This is one of the more interesting areas in the game, due to the many conveyors on which Mega Man must ride. There are three of these suckers, and each travels a more complicated path than the one before. Getting on board the rolling platform is easy. Staying on it while being attacked from all sides is a trick. The metal-blade weapon, which can shoot at an angle, is especially useful here. Don't let the spinning spools near you, and you'll make it to the top.

Later in this world, you'll have to choose one of several ladders to climb. There's no wrong choice. Which ladder you choose depends on the special equipment (levitation platforms, etc.) you've got and which items in this area you want to obtain. Be sure to go for the one-up at the top of the highest ladder.

At the end of this level, you'll face Crash Man. He tosses crash bombs, which explode on the ground, usually at your feet. He's a tough opponent until you get the right rhythm. Here's what to do: Every time Crash Man throws a bomb, jump over it. When you jump, he jumps. Blast him in the air. When you land, jump over his next bomb. Continue this pattern until you defeat this mad bomber.

Metal Man

In this mechanized world, you must cross conveyor belts that are trying to drop you into the deadly depths of a giant machine. The conveyors may be moving either left or right. When you jump on a conveyor, be prepared to be dragged in one direction or the other. If the conveyor is moving left, run or hop to advance. If it's moving right, ride with it. Be careful when leaping from a left-moving conveyor to a right-moving one. If you're still running when you hit the right-moving one, your speed, combined with the belt's forward motion, will zip you off the other end.

One area in this world contains metal screws that wind continually through the floors and ceilings. They try their darnedest to twist their way into your soft and pliable innards.

The screws are easy to destroy, but they keep coming. Believe it or not, that's good news. Why? Because when you kill an enemy, he sometimes leaves behind an energy capsule or maybe even a one-up. Take a corridor swarming with easy-to-kill, unlimited-in-number enemies and combine that with some battle time, and what do you get? Full energy meters.

After fighting the screws (sounds like something you do in a prison, doesn't it?) and going through the gear room, where the gear clowns reside, you'll enter Metal Man's area. His frantic leaping and his metal-blade weapon make him a formidable opponent. Stay close and jump over his blades. Practice is the key.

Heat Man

In Heat Man's world, you must leap from rock to rock, praying that you don't tumble into a pool of lava. (Deep-fried Mega Man anyone?) Worse, the only way to scale some walls is to leap onto platforms that have an annoying habit of disappearing exactly when you need them. As the clockmaker says, it's just a matter of timing. Learn the precise moment to jump, and the platforms will appear before you fall. Usually. You can blast some walls in this area with crash bombs, but don't count on that to save you.

Some lava beds are huge. You can usually cross them by leaping from rock to rock, but use the jet sled instead. It makes your trip a lot more enjoyable, not to mention safer. Your levitation platform will provide valuable assistance in some areas, too. I'm assuming you've already obtained this special equipment. If you haven't, maybe you should try playing the levels in a different order, eh?

Eventually, you'll run into Heat Man. If you know the right weapon to use, beating him is a cinch. If you don't . . . .

Flash Man

Most video games these days include an ice level. The makers of *Mega Man 2* felt no need to break the tradition. Flash Man's world contains enough crystallized water to sink the Titanic. Walk carefully. This stuff is slippery.

All things considered, this is an easy level. The most difficult task is finding the best route through the maze. However, the maze is simple, and there's more than one correct route. As usual, which route you choose depends on your supplies. One exit, for example, requires a supply of crash bombs.

Flash Man is no Chuck Norris. You'll cream him easily enough. Stay close and fire rapidly.

Wood Man

The above-ground area of Wood Man's domain will give you no difficulty, but when you descend into the caves, you'll face the hot dogs, and I do mean hot. These guys shoot streams of deadly fire. Jump precisely so the fire will pass beneath you; then immediately jump again and shoot the hot dog in the face. It'll take a few hits to discourage these puppies.

In Wood Man's world, the diagonally shooting metal-blade weapon is again a great help, especially where you must climb down the ladders. At the foot of the ladders are creatures mean enough to suck the marrow from your bones. With the metal-blade weapon, you can, in some cases, blast the trouble makers without leaving the relative safety of the ladder.

In my opinion, Wood Man is the toughest boss of the eight. It'll take several attempts to beat him. His leaf shield is almost impenetrable and is extremely dangerous when thrown. Avoid the leaves (like you needed me to tell you that, right?) and keep blasting. You'll get him.

Quick Man

Quick Man's realm is one of the most challenging. Around virtually every bend is an energy beam. Hesitate in its path, and it'll blast you into cosmic dust. One long, vertical area is particularly difficult. You must steer Mega Man through this area as he falls, timing your moves with precision. You'll need to experiment to learn the shortest path, so plan on practicing.

There is an easier way to get past the energy beams. Rather than tell you outright, let me ask you a question: Can you freeze time?

Quick Man is a demon of a fighter. The only tricks are to use the right weapon and practice.

Skull Castle

Hey, you made it! Congratulations! Now for the bad news: you've got a long way to go, not to mention several new bosses to beat. Oh yeah, did I mention that you have to fight all eight original bosses again? Stiff upper lip and all that.

The first area in Skull Castle is deceptively simple. But don't relax. The fun is yet to come. For example, you'll arrive at a room with a ladder. So what? Well, the ladder is so high above your head that even Magic Johnson couldn't reach it. Getting to that ladder is as frustrating as typing with your toes. Here's how: use three levitation platforms and practice, practice, practice. Don't give up.

After climbing the ladder, you'll enter a room with a deep pit. The only way over is to leap from block to block. This is a tricky enough stunt without having to deal with the dragon that'll pop up behind you. Don't slow down; stay ahead of old sulfur breath. When you get to the end of the room, you'll have your chance to turn the tables. Use the right weapon. Also, stand on the highest of the blocks. That way, if the dragon hits you, you'll land on the block below, rather than plunging to your death.

Next is a sweat-popping jet-sled cruise over a spike-covered floor. At the end of your ride, climb the ladder on the far right, a move that requires precise control. The jet sled has barely enough energy to get you to the ladder. It'll vaporize almost the instant you jump. Don't miss the ladder unless you have a fondness for things sharp and pointy.

Soon you'll enter an area similar to Metal Man's world, where screws bore through the floor and ceiling. As before, this is a good place to build up your energy and maybe grab a one-up.

One challenging area in Skull Castle is the room in which the walls change into attack machines. For the best chance of survival, memorize which blocks transform, as well as the order in which they do it. Having a couple of "E" capsules isn't a bad idea, either.

You'll be pleased to know (ha ha) that Skull Castle contains an underwater area, similar to Bubble Man's world, well stocked with lethal spiked mines. Jump over the mines while avoiding the chomping jaws of giant fish. Then, enter a vertical passageway whose walls are lined with mines. Carefully steer Mega Man as he falls. One bad turn, and he'll be skewered like a cocktail frank.

You'll next battle a new boss, Guts-Dozer. This guy's tough. When he appears, jump onto the flat area above his treads and in front of his fist. Use the right weapon (hint: it's something you throw) and shoot him in the eyes.

Trap doors in the next area will drop you onto enemies, or worse, onto spikes. Learn where they are and avoid them.

Unfortunately, you can't avoid the conveyor rides. These conveyors, which are much more complicated than the ones in Crash Man's world, require thought and planning to master. In order to stay on the rolling platform, avoid the spinning spools and jump over the blocks under which only the platform can pass. The leaf shield will keep enemies at bay, but nothing can protect you from the bed of spikes if you lose your footing.

In the final room use crash bombs to bust open walls. Until you destroy the walls, you can't reach the machines behind them. Again, think and plan; you can't waste even a single bomb. Destroy only those walls absolutely necessary to destroy. Use a levitation platform to get over others.

Now the fun really begins. (Tired yet?) In the transporter room are eight transporters, each of which brings you face to face with one of the original eight bosses. You must defeat all eight again. Use the same weapons and strategies that were effective the first time.

After you beat the eight bosses, a new transporter materializes. This one takes you to Dr. Wily. When he appears, blast the windshield of his vehicle, jumping over his shots as you do. When the windshield is history, concentrate on Dr. Wily himself. He'll run like the coward he is.

Wily will return, though. The final battle is deep in the dungeons of Skull Castle, where you must survive a long corridor of dripping lava. At the end of the corridor, Dr. Wily waits, desperate and mean. Only one weapon harms Dr. Wily. You're going to have to be a *Super* Nintendo Master Gamer to cool this guy's heels. Go for it!

Teenage Mutant Ninja Turtles

Company: *Ultra*
Type: *Arcade Search, Rescue, and Destroy*

The Game

Objective: To rescue April and Splinter, then destroy Shredder and his followers.

Organization: The game is set in the streets and sewers of New York. Although there are some overhead views, most of the game consists of horizontally scrolling action scenes. You'll have to make it through six levels.

Creatures: Your enemies include Foot Soldiers, fire freaks, roof leapers, roller cars, and searchlight mechanisms, not to mention the bosses—Bebop, Rocksteady, Mouser, Meka Turtle, the Technodrome, and Shredder.

General Strategy: Unlike most video games, in *Teenage Mutant Ninja Turtles* you have four different characters to choose from, each of which is available for turtle duty at any time. Learn each turtle's strengths, and switch between them as appropriate. Know your enemies well. Only then can you make intelligent decisions as to which turtle to enter into the fight.

The Controls

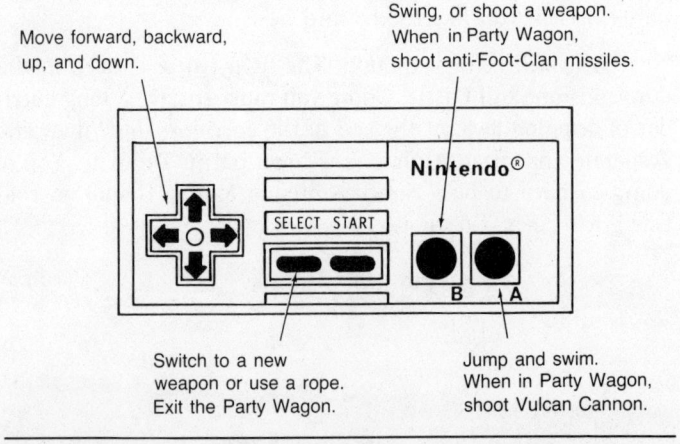

Move forward, backward, up, and down.

Swing, or shoot a weapon. When in Party Wagon, shoot anti-Foot-Clan missiles.

Switch to a new weapon or use a rope. Exit the Party Wagon.

Jump and swim. When in Party Wagon, shoot Vulcan Cannon.

The Challenge

Who would've thought that a group of comic-book characters with an absurd name like Teenage Mutant Ninja Turtles would become a national phenomenon? What a strange world we live in! One thing is for sure, Turtlemania is sweeping the country —comic books, novels, cartoon shows, action figures, and now their own full-length feature film!

The video game version for your NES does a beautiful job of capturing these radical reptiles in action. If you've always wondered what it would be like to be a Teenage Mutant Ninja Turtle, now's your chance to find out.

Strategies

Keep a close watch on your turtles' health. When the turtle gets weak, immediately switch to another. You can heal a weak turtle. A dead turtle is, well, a dead turtle.

When you find pizza in an easily accessible location, heal all four turtles. Remember, in most cases, when you exit and then re-enter a building (or sewer), your bonus items, including pizzas, are restocked.

Each of the four turtles has his strengths and weaknesses. The following list ranks the turtles from best to worst in five important categories:

Weapon strength:	Don, Raph, Leo, Mike
Weapon reach:	Don, Leo, Mike, Raph
Weapon speed:	Raph, Mike, Leo, Don
Weapon defense:	Leo, Mike, Raph, Don
Run and Jump:	Equal

Overall, Don is the strongest turtle, so keep him healthy and use him often. In addition to being a powerful offensive weapon, Don's bo (the fighting stick) can provide excellent protection, once you get used to using it. In fact, when crouching and swinging down, Don is completely protected from a frontal attack.

Although Leo's weapon is weak, his reach is about equal to Don's. Moreover, his horizontal swings shield him from overhead attacks. Use Leo in tight situations when Don's strength is low.

Both Mike and Raph have limited offensive range. In addition, they cannot attack downward. Use them in less dangerous situations, saving Don and Leo for the more challenging fights.

Level 1

Once you learn which sewers to avoid, this level is a cinch. There are only three sewers you actually need to enter. Enemies of all types infest the underground chambers here, but except for the bosses, most are easy prey. Learn which weapon (and which turtle) is most effective against each creature, and then switch when necessary.

In one sewer, you'll find pizza. Pizza is important not only because it's the turtles' favorite food, but also because it restores the turtles' strength. Remember, when you return to a building, the pizzas get restocked. Take all the pizza you need.

In this level, you must beat two bosses—Bebop and Rocksteady. Use Don to attack Bebop, staying to the left to give yourself plenty of jumping room. When Bebop attacks, jump over him, stabbing downward from above. While Bebop is on the ground, attack him from a distance.

Once you beat Bebop, Rocksteady and April will flee to another room. When you catch up with them, fight Rocksteady the same way you fought Bebop.

Level 2

Here, you must defuse eight bombs before they blow up a dam. Sound easy? Did I mention that you have only a couple of minutes to get the job done?

Several hazards will slow your progress. Avoid the single electric beams by timing your moves. The double beams, however, are sure to get you. Some seaweed here is electrified, as well. Some you can avoid, but the larger patches will zap you no matter how careful you are. Watch for the strangler vines. If you get tangled in them, you can't get away.

In this level use your weakest turtle first—switch turtles the instant his strength gets low. Follow this strategy, and you'll start level three with your best fighters ready to go.

Level 3

When you appear in the city, climb into the Party Wagon, then head left and up. The first building with an open door contains pizza and missiles. You can enter and exit this building as often as you like. Heal your turtles completely. Grab at least 11 missiles.

Now climb back into the Party Wagon and head south. Find two buildings, side by side, both with open doors. Enter the building on the right (the tall one), and get the scroll weapon. If you plan on completing the game, get 20 to 40 scrolls for each turtle. In the basement are treacherous water passages that contain yummy pizza snacks. If you fall into the water, it'll drag you outside to the street.

After stocking up, continue south. When you've gone as far as possible (make sure you cross a short bridge), travel east. When you can go no farther, head north. Cross two bridges, go around a U-shaped street, cross another bridge (heading south), then ride west. (Feeling a little car sick?) After another bridge, you'll find a single building.

Use Leo here, since his weapon can hit flying enemies from both above and below. When in the sewers, use short jumps to get over the water passages. Don't fight the robot enemies. Instead, wait for them to fall into the water. At the end of this area, you'll find a pizza. Exit and re-enter the sewer as often as necessary to heal all four turtles.

You emerge from the sewer in front of a single building. Enter the building and battle your way through to the end, where you'll face the dastardly Meka Turtle. At first, this guy looks like you. Use Don to fight him. After you hit Meka a few times, he sheds his disguise and attacks in his true form. Beat him in order to rescue master Splinter. Cowabunga, dudes!

 By the way, in the level 3 city, there's a building in which you can rescue a captured turtle.

Level 4

Level 4 is long and treacherous. You'll face many new obstacles—lasers, magnets, and spiked floors, to name a few. Keep a close watch on your turtles' health. At the beginning of area 1 (the walls are marked with numbers) is a full pizza. Use it to heal all four turtles. Starting this level with a set of weak turtles would be foolish indeed.

You can skip some areas here. Unfortunately, this level is too complicated to describe in detail, so you'll have to do some exploring. Suffice it to say that, no matter which route you choose, you'll have your work cut out for you. Practice. And make sure you find ropes—you'll need them to cross between buildings.

On the final approach to Big Mouser, you'll pass through two rooms with moving walls. Drop through the small openings in the floor. Don't waste time, and don't try to grab pizzas or weapons.

Big Mouser is easy to kill. Stand in front of him, centered, so the laser blasts miss you. When Big Mouser opens his mouth, shoot up, hitting the target there.

Level 5

This level consists of three underground passages and two buildings. The Technodrome, the boss for this level, is in one of the three passages. Which passage? Well, that's a bit of a problem. Whenever you start the game, the Technodrome is randomly placed. You need to explore.

As you move between passages and buildings, avoid helicopters with searchlights. If they see you, guards will attack. Inside the building closest to where you begin this level is a half pizza. Re-enter the building as often as needed to restore your turtles' strength. If one of your turtles was captured, you can find him here. Ignore the second building unless you need weapons.

After healing your turtles, hunt for the Technodrome. The three passages vary in difficulty, so start with the easiest one. How do you know which is easiest? By playing, of course!

To beat the Technodrome, shoot its eye when it opens. Before you can do that, however, you need to take out its defenses—the front field generator, the hatch, and the guns. Don't bother with the rear field generator. It poses no threat.

Whatever you do, don't get run over by the Technodrome. It'll mess you up something awful.

Level 6

Your final mission takes place inside a large building infested with tough enemies. Before you get to Shredder, you'll face such awesome creatures as space men with laser guns and huge lizards. Avoid fighting whenever possible. Run! One thing is certain—if your turtles haven't eaten much pizza lately, they probably won't make it.

Amazingly enough, Shredder is so easy to beat it's almost a rip-off. Blast him with scrolls. As long as you keep hitting him, he's helpless.

Pizza time!

ACTION & SPORTS

Action and Sports

Batman

Company: Sunsoft
Type: Arcade

The Game

Objective: To destroy the The Joker's gang, which threatens Gotham City, and then face The Joker himself in Gotham City Cathedral.

Organization: Batman is broken down into five levels. Each level is divided into a number of vertically and horizontally scrolling stages representing various locations in Gotham City.

Creatures: Most of the lesser enemies—mobile trackers, jaders, railrunners, drop claws, and others—are easy to dispatch. The level bosses, however, are increasingly more difficult. They're equipped with strong firepower, and it takes several more shots to kill them. The bosses are Killer Moth, Electrocutioner, Machine Intelligence System, Dual-Container Alarm, Firebug, and . . . The Joker.

General Strategy: Keep one eye on your enemies and the other on your life meter. If you happen to have a third eye, make sure your weapon count stays at or near 99, the maximum. Beating an end boss sometimes requires an entire cache of weapons. The weapons at your disposal include the basic punch (for close-up battles), the batarang (which reduces your weapon count by one each time it's used), the spear gun (which reduces your weapon count by two), and the triple-threat dirk (which reduces your weapon count by three). Use the least powerful weapon that'll do the job. Otherwise, you'll risk having too little strength to beat the tough guys.

The Controls

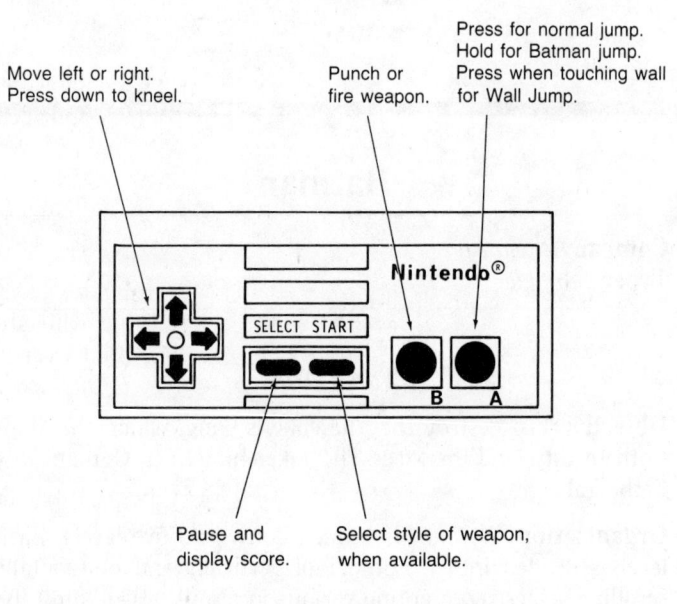

The Challenge

If the box-office receipts are any indication, you've probably seen the Warner Bros. movie, *Batman*. The video game version of this blockbuster does a good job of capturing the film's dark and dangerous atmosphere. But don't be surprised if you see a couple unfamiliar faces.

The game offers some high-quality graphics and is very playable. The only problem is that the Batman character is a little difficult to control at times, particularly when he's clinging to a wall. When using this move, it takes great skill to keep Batman from slipping and falling into the clutches of his evil enemies. Hey, nobody said that climbing walls is easy.

Strategies

Don't be discouraged if you're not immediately successful in a particular level. You'll need to fine-tune your jumps and shots before you can escape some scenes unscathed. Try different tactics; they may work.

If you're using turbo-fire, your adversaries may seem more aggressive than with manual shooting. Try adjusting your turbo-fire setting to less than full speed.

When your life or weapons dwindle, find a spot with a constant flow of bad guys. Kill them as they attack and scoop up the icons they leave behind.

Stage 1-1

This level is a good place to build your weapon cache and to practice killing bad guys. You can hit some enemies before they get right beside you. Moreover, backtracking will often bring enemies back to life. Use this method to gather weapons and to heal yourself.

Stage 1-2

This level, set in the streets of Gotham City, features the mobile home mines, nasty devices that zip towards you and explode when they get close. In order to avoid them, learn how close you can get before they explode, then either jump over them or leap back.

When you see Heatwave on the stair-like platforms, either destroy him and his higher twin or avoid them by climbing the walls. Keep in mind, however, that if you climb the walls, you may slip and fall back to the ground. When this happens, you're at the mercy of your enemies—at least for a while.

Before the end of stage 1-2, you'll face your first major obstacle—The Enforcer. To get past this jet-pack-equipped character, crouch on the left side of a pillar and fire at him when he glides into range. Once you've dispatched The Enforcer, *don't* relax. You still have one more to beat.

The last obstacle is somewhat hidden. After dropping to the street, you'll find a guard leaning against a building. If you get too close, he'll attack with his sword, so shoot him from a distance. Also, be sure you have plenty of head room—if the guard charges, you'll want to leap over him.

Stage 1-3

Outside City Hall you'll encounter Killer Moth, the level 1 boss. Killer starts on the right side and flies left towards you. Get your punch ready and stand your ground. He'll cruise over your head, then head back to the right, where he'll hover and fire. After this, he'll skim along the road toward you. Punch him as he approaches. No sweat! A few good punches, and Killer Moth turns into Killed Moth.

Stage 2-1

The Axis Chemical Factory is a good place to rebuild your strength. Here, you'll also get lots of jumping practice, due to the many platforms you must cross. During your travels watch out for gluk, a lethal chemical that drips from above and forms pools on the floor.

After you defeat the first mobile tracker, you must make a long jump over some dangerous chemicals. To make this jump, use a move I call the drop-grab-jump. It works like this—drop off the edge of the platform, grab the side as you're falling, and jump over to your destination. Drop, grab, jump. Get it?

Stage 2-2

The power room holds few enemies, but it's no free ride. You'll have to do a lot of clinging and jumping. To make matters worse, some areas of the power room have electric ceilings. So when you jump, use a quick tap on button B. If you jump too high, you'll be sporting a new hairdo. (I don't think the static look is in this year.)

The biggest hazard in Stage 2-2 is the maze of platforms and electrical obstacles that winds through the power room. Bounce between the walls and platforms, slaying the prowling bad guys as you go. In addition to bouncing, use the famous drop-grab-jump routine where appropriate.

Stage 2-3

The drop claw, which spits smart bombs, is your first challenge here. Don't be surprised if your weapon supply gets low. Stand under them, slightly to the left or right, and punch the bombs as they fall. Collect icons as they appear in order to rebuild your supplies. Then vamoose. The safest way to exit is to punch three bombs in a row. If you ignore the icons that appear, the bombs will stop falling until the icons vanish. This is your chance for a safe getaway.

   Later, make like electricity—take the path of least resistance. If there's a safe route around something, use it. There's no point in taking unnecessary risks. (Try this with the second heatwave.)

Stage 2-4

The Machine Intelligence System, which controls all the devices in this section, will challenge your gaming skills to the max. Here's how to beat it: When it shoots, jump over the lower pair of bullets and duck under the higher pair. Then, between its shots, attack with your spear gun.

Once past the guns, you must destroy the blinking electric current controller on the left. Stand to the left of the electrical pillar, near the right side of the screen. (If you sit on the conveyor belt, it's difficult to control your shots and avoid the toxic drips.) Jump and shoot to take out the controller. When it's gone, immediately drop to the platform below. If you don't, you'll get socked from behind.

Now comes the part that separates the Nintendo Master Gamers from the wimps. Switch to your punch in order to conserve weapon power. When the nerve center on the right fires, jump up, get as close as you can, and crouch. Wait till it fires again, then stand, punch, and return to a crouch. Repeat the move as often as necessary. See? No machine can stand up to Batman.

Stage 3-1

Now it's into the underground sewers, in search of a secret cave. First, fight a group of springing creatures called jaders. Load up your batarang and time your throws so you hit the jaders when they land. If you don't want to get creamed by these leaping losers, run in the opposite direction of their jumps. If you don't, they'll pounce on you repeatedly. Ouch!

Use batarangs to dispatch any heatwaves you may run into. Remember, contact with the turbines can be hazardous to your health.

After fighting more jaders, it's on to . . .

Stage 3-2

Hope you're not afraid of heights, because you'll have to negotiate some frighteningly long drops. A word of warning: Don't jump straight down, or you'll land on a turbine.

After the second heatwave, drop to the right, avoiding the turbines, and take on a pair of jaders. If you don't move too far forward after the first jader appears, you won't have to fight them at the same time.

Stage 3-3

Here you'll meet the EEV, a large rolling robot that shoots fireballs. The best way to eliminate this bucket of bolts is to back up until its shots disappear. When you move forward again . . . hey, it's gone! If your conscience won't let you take the easy way out, try this: Get as close as you can to the EEV, crouch, and punch or shoot it when it comes into range.

Don't miss a jump or get knocked from a platform. If you fall, you have to refight some meanies.

Stage 3-4

Yikes! It's the Electrocutioner! This guy's a dangerous foe with a moon attacker beam weapon and a shocking personality (sorry). To survive his wrath, move immediately to the room's center and load up with batarangs. Fling them as fast as possible. Before you can say "Batman battles baddies best," this member of The Joker's menagerie will be toast. You'll finish with little strength, but the Electrocutioner will be forever nighty-night.

Stage 4-1

The Laboratory Ruins, The Joker's backup hideout, houses many familiar opponents, but in greater numbers than ever before. If your offensive strategies are weak, expect trouble. Hint: Don't let the patterned background hide lurking mobile-home mines.

Stage 4-2

Here, you can use the drop-grab-jump move again (thanks to the many blocks situated below low ceilings). Luckily, the timing isn't as critical as before. Miss grabbing a platform, though, and it's the old gear-grind for Batman.

What? How do you get past the chest-high gears in the wall? It's easy. Get near the gears, jump up, and cling to the wall on the left. Quickly leap to the right, and you'll be at . . .

Stage 4-3

Look at that! You can see the exit sign. Can this level be that easy? Hardly. You're about to learn a whole new meaning of the words "scenic route."

Drop down and you'll find a rail runner. Don't bother fighting him. Take the detour around him and avoid the damage. What's this? A rail runner and a drop claw? You can handle it. Go right, to avoid the drop claw's bombs.

More drop claws coming up. Get almost underneath each one, then let the soldiers come to you. No point in contending with both soldiers and bombs, is there?

Stage 4-4

The dual-container alarm is one tough cookie. Okay, *two* tough cookies! Climb atop the middle platform, then turn to the left, and start slugging. Once you destroy one alarm box, the remaining box goes to the lower right corner. If you stay on top of the platform, you'll get shot, so follow the box to the floor. Select the spear gun, then crouch and fire until you destroy the second alarm.

It's a tough battle, but you'll survive—barely.

Stage 5-1

Your jumping skills are critical. Blocks and gigantic gears wind upwards through the thermal processing plant. You must avoid the gears, as well as the heatwaves and javelins. If you've mastered the mid-jump punch, use it to clear a path—jump, punch, then reattach Batman to the wall.

Your drop-grab-jump maneuver will help you get past some hanging gears. Still, some areas are impossible to complete without sustaining damage. Enter this stage only with a full life force.

Stage 5-2

Here you are—Gotham City Cathedral. But before you meet The Joker, you must kill his sidekick, Firebug, a formidable enemy armed with 600-million-degree fireballs. (Who brought the marshmallows?) Ready your batarang, slide as far to the left as possible, then leap over the fireballs as they appear. After each jump, just before you hit the ground, launch a batarang. Continue until Firebug explodes.

Stage 5-3

Finally, it's The Joker! In this, the ultimate, battle, two strategies will help you survive:

1. To dodge his bullets, learn when The Joker is going to shoot.
2. Punch only when you're standing still (The Joker can then move *through* you without causing damage).

In order to strike The Joker without getting creamed by his shots or by the lightning bolts, crouch where his gun meets the floor. Blast him good, and it'll be The Joker who finds himself lying on the pavement outside the Cathedral!

Double Dragon II: The Revenge

Company: *Acclaim*
Type: *Martial Arts Action*

The Game

Objective: To destroy the Black Shadow Warriors and take on their leader, the mastermind.

Organization: *Double Dragon II: The Revenge* is broken down into eight missions (nine, if you play the Supreme Master level). Most of these missions consist of vertically or horizontally scrolling scenes. You'll battle through the inner city, the heliport, the undersea base, the Forest of Death, the Mansion of Terror, and other exciting locales.

Creatures: Your enemies are the Black Shadow Warriors—a group of thugs, muggers, hoods, greasers, street chicks, giants, and androbots intent on taking over the city.

General Strategy: As a martial arts master, you have an array of devastating moves, including punches, kicks, and grabs. Master all moves, especially the powerful ones like the spinning cyclone and the high jump kick. Learn which moves are most effective on which enemies. In addition, know your enemies' moves. Be prepared when they appear.

The Controller

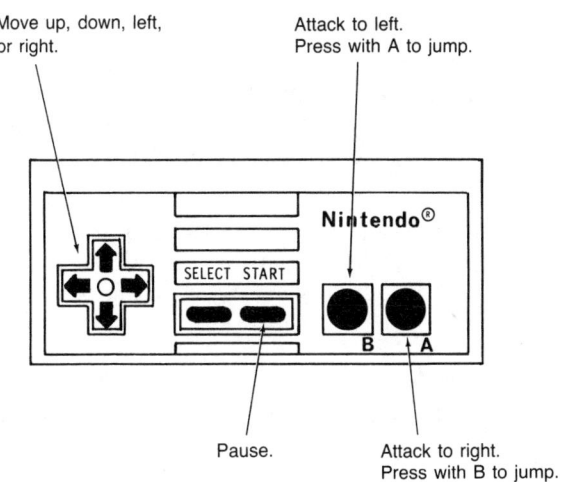

The Challenge

Although many martial arts games are available for the NES, they don't feature the realistic battle sequences and smooth gameplay of the *Double Dragon* series. The original *Double Dragon*, which gained immense popularity in the coin arcades before its move to home computers and video game machines, was an instant success. And it now appears that its sequel, *Double Dragon II: The Revenge*, will follow in its footsteps. Simply put, here's a karate game you can really sink your fists into.

Got that NES plugged in? Let's pulverize some Shadow Warriors!

Strategies

Every mission in *Double Dragon II* is packed with enemies, and each attacks in his own way. Learn your enemies' strengths and weaknesses, then plan your strategy. In addition, memorize when and from where enemies attack. For example, if a street chick must climb down a ladder in order to join the fight, wait for her at the bottom. Punch her out before she gets to the ground.

Keep in mind that anything that can kill you can kill your opponent too. If you're fighting near a spike-covered pit, force your enemy into it. If a thug drops a weapon, pick it up and use it. If there's a live grenade on the ground, lure your enemy over it. In other words, if you tend to think of deadly obstacles as things to avoid, you had better shift your thinking in *Double Dragon II*.

Want to start out with extra lives? Choose the two-player mode and kill your ally—you'll then get all his lives. (Some friend you are!) To punish you for your crime, the game gets much tougher, so the extra lives give you little advantage in the long run.

Mission 1: Into the Turf

Mission 1 is little more than a training ground. Here you'll learn to anticipate your enemies' attacks and to take the initiative in battle. In addition, you'll be introduced to several types of enemies—enemies that will appear again and again throughout the game. Mastering the techniques required to complete this level will take you a long way toward ultimate victory.

Generally, the warriors here attack in pairs. Be aggressive. Advance on your opponent. Punch or kick him down before his partner attacks. Waste no moves. Slow fighters end up as the meat in a Black Shadow Warrior sandwich.

When you get to the ladder, wait at the bottom for the street chicks. Punch or kick while they're still on the ladder. The battle will be half over before they even take a swing. Similarly, when near an elevator, wait near the door. When it opens, surprise your opponents with a flurry of punches.

A word of warning: stay away from ledges. If you get knocked off, you'll lose a life.

This level's boss is a big guy with an iron constitution. In other words, he can absorb a lot of punches. To beat him, move in, punch three or four times, then back off. If you're timing is right, he won't get a chance to grab you by the throat. (Gag, gasp, choke.)

Mission 2: At the Heliport

Here, just like in Mission 1, the warriors tend to attack in pairs. This time, however, rather than charging from opposite sides, they approach together from the same direction. Believe it or not, this gives you an advantage. With a well-timed kick or two, you can take out both enemies at once. Are you tough or what?

This level contains many dangerous ledges. Don't fall or get thrown off. The enemies usually attack from the right, so move quickly forward to meet them. If you let the battle come to you, you risk being flung from the ledge.

Climb the last ladder to the top of the heliport and immediately climb back down again. Why? A helicopter will fly in from the right with guns blazing. If you're at the bottom of the ladder, most, if not all, of the bullets will miss you. If you stay at the top, the Black Shadow Warriors will be adding swiss cheese to their sandwiches.

When the helicopter stops firing, warriors start attacking from the ladder. Stand to the right of the ladder, and punch the enemies as they descend. Watch out for grenades!

At the top, after exchanging punches with a few wimpy warriors, you'll meet the bosses, two ninjas whose spinning and jumping antics will put your martial arts skills to the test. Use your spinning cyclone kick and jump-kick. Above all, don't get discouraged. Practice.

Mission 3: Battle in the Chopper

This is the shortest level in the game. In fact, it's only one room. Unfortunately, the room is in a helicopter, flying high over the city. Worse, this helicopter's door opens at the worst times, sucking everything in the chopper out toward the wild blue yonder. Too bad you didn't bring a parachute, huh?

When fighting the first few warriors, stay to the left, away from the outside door. These warriors are too weak to force you out when the door opens, but the suction from the door is dangerous. Fight normally. Just keep away from that door.

When the big guys attack, get all the way to the right, in the corner farthest from the door. This helps you in two ways. First, if your opponent throws you over his shoulder, you'll be tossed away from the outside door rather than towards it. Second, when the door opens, the big guy will get sucked out. He's too slow to avoid the big fall. Look out below!

Mission 4: The Undersea Base

The first warriors here throw chains. Avoid the chains by moving forward or back (up or down on the screen). Don't forget that you can use weapons too. Pick them up when you can. If you don't have a weapon, move in close, punching and kicking.

After taking the elevator down, you'll be in a corridor with a low ceiling. No jump kicks allowed here. If you try, you'll bang your head on the ceiling, leaving you stunned and vulnerable. Warriors here approach from alternate sides. Move forward to fight the first enemy. Then turn and advance on the second, who comes up from behind. After dealing with him, turn yet again to face the third. Punch fast, and you'll always get in the first licks.

As you advance, watch your head. You don't want to get minced by the spiked booby traps.

After demolishing the last group of warriors, you'll be on a moving treadmill. Keep walking. If you stop, the treadmill will drag you off the ledge. To get to the other side, move down off the treadmill and jump to the left. Then move up onto the second treadmill, and go through the door.

Mission 5: The Forest of Death

You'll meet many familiar enemies here. Don't be shy about using their weapons against them. Watch out for the ledge. Walk off the right-hand side to get to the next level down, but don't jump. Blind jumps can be hazardous to your health.

After descending the ladder and whomping some punk ladies, cross the river. Plan your jumps carefully, aligning yourself front to back and left to right with the stepping stones.

Kill the enemies descending the vines, then climb up to the top of the ledge. At the top fight from the right side. The left ledge is a killer.

Now move to the right and take out two knife-wielding ninjas. Beat these two guys, and the boss, a giant locomotive, will move onto the screen. Climb up to the locomotive's door by jumping on the treads and pipes. Watch out for the steam.

When you get to the door, the locomotive stops moving and warriors attack. Be prepared for dynamite. Lure your enemies into the blast, but keep yourself at a cool distance. When the big guy appears, lure him down to the ground. If you can stay one level above or below him, he won't be able to land a punch. But you will.

Mission 6: Mansion of Terror

With practice, you can get to mission 6 with little difficulty. In fact, after mastering the first five levels, you can get here without losing a life. From mission 6 on, however, things get tough. Not only must you defeat many Black Shadow Warriors, but you must also deal with some dangerous traps.

For example, when you first enter the Mansion of Terror, you'll be standing before a spiked floor. The only way to cross this prickly carpet is by jumping on the disappearing platforms. Jump too slowly, and your yucky insides will decorate the razor-sharp knives. To add to the excitement, the torches here drip deadly bits of fire that can both injure you and knock you off your feet. Deadly stuff, indeed! What to do? Try this: wait for the lowest platform to appear. Then cross in only two jumps.

After the first set of vanishing platforms (that's right, folks—there are more), the Black Shadow Warriors will attack.

Lure the enemy onto the center platform, drop to the floor, and attack with kicks from below.

Things get really tough now. First, move to the left as far as you can, so that all the disappearing platforms are on the screen. Now, study the pattern in which the platforms appear and disappear. Got it? Take a deep breath and start jumping. Needless to say, the timing is extremely critical. How critical? One person I know sacrificed six of his favorite games to the video gods and still never got past mission 6.

Mission 7: The Trap Room

You made it? Wow! I'm impressed. You just may be a Nintendo Master Gamer, after all. Don't get smug, though. The fun has just begun.

In mission 7, you must first cross three moving conveyors. Before jumping onto a conveyor, take note of the direction in which it's moving, so you don't get dragged off onto the spikes when you land. In addition, carefully calculate the length of your jumps. Believe me, missing a conveyor is not in your best interests. Jumping from the left side of the first conveyor should get you safely to the second. Getting to the third conveyor takes experimentation and practice—it requires much greater accuracy.

After the conveyors, you'll take on more Black Shadow Warriors. Fight efficiently. The floor here vanishes segment by segment. If you don't defeat your opponents before the floor is gone, it's the old spikes-through-the-guts for you. Lure your enemies into their own dynamite blasts. These guys are *so* stupid.

In the last room, expect knife-wielding punks, dynamite-throwing thugs, sword-swinging ninjas, and more. In other words, although the enemies here are nothing new, you'll face them in overwhelming numbers. Use your toughest punches and kicks. You can't afford to play patty-face.

Mission 8: The Double Illusion

Slipping and sliding! This level features ice-covered floors that make it hard to fight and that can easily slide you off into a pit. In the first room, move all the way to the right and about halfway down the screen. From this position, you can kick your enemies onto the spiked floor.

In the next room, after fighting a few more Black Shadow Warriors, take the ladder down, but be careful when you get to the bottom. If you climb down too fast, you'll slide across the floor and off the edge. On this icy floor, you'll battle three big guys. Hope you're as tough as you think.

In the last room, first confront four ninjas who leap around like rabbits on hot coals. These guys will make you dizzy with their crazy antics. They're hard to hit, but once you get one on the ground, stand over him and punch him the instant he stands—no mercy!

With the ninjas down, you have only one warrior left to beat. Surprise! It's your shadow come to life! Use hyper uppercuts and high jump kicks. When he jumps, attack with a spinning cyclone kick. Watch out for fire balls.

Once you beat your shadow, you're finished with the Warrior level of play. Now move on to the Supreme Master level, where you'll fight through all eight missions again. After that, you get to face the mysterious ninth mission. Good luck!

World Championship Wrestling

Company: *FCI*
Type: *Wrestling Simulation*

The Game

Objective: To fight your way to the top and become the World Championship Wrestling (WCW) champion.

Organization: Each of 11 rounds of mad wrestling action takes place in the WCW ring, with side-view perspective.

Creatures: Creatures? Yeah, that describes your opponents. For example, take a look at the Road Warriors—Hawk and Animal. Yikes! You'll battle 13 WCW wrestlers, every one a creature, before you can wear the championship belt.

General Strategy: Read the game manual before starting, and memorize your moves. The standard maneuvers—punching, kicking, and running—are important, but you must understand all moves, offensive and defensive, in order to win consistently. Use your wrestler's specialty move only against a weak opponent. Otherwise, you'll likely end up on the mat yourself, a humiliating position for a Nintendo Master Gamer.

The Controls

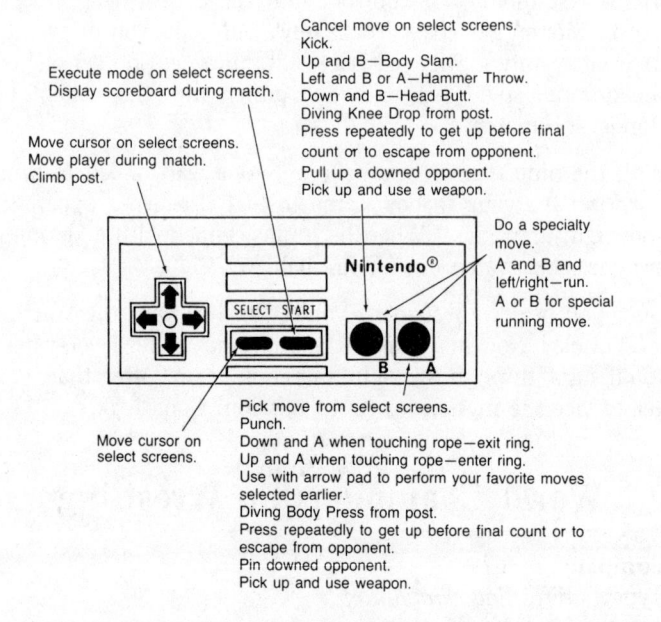

Execute mode on select screens.
Display scoreboard during match.

Move cursor on select screens.
Move player during match.
Climb post.

Cancel move on select screens.
Kick.
Up and B—Body Slam.
Left and B or A—Hammer Throw.
Down and B—Head Butt.
Diving Knee Drop from post.
Press repeatedly to get up before final count or to escape from opponent.
Pull up a downed opponent.
Pick up and use a weapon.

Do a specialty move.
A and B and left/right—run.
A or B for special running move.

Move cursor on select screens.

Pick move from select screens.
Punch.
Down and A when touching rope—exit ring.
Up and A when touching rope—enter ring.
Use with arrow pad to perform your favorite moves selected earlier.
Diving Body Press from post.
Press repeatedly to get up before final count or to escape from opponent.
Pin downed opponent.
Pick up and use weapon.

The Challenge

World Championship Wrestling, like other sports simulations, differs from most video games in this book. First, the concept of "levels" rarely applies to sport games, unless you consider a wrestling match or an inning in a baseball game to be a level. Second, strategies for sports games are more general. In this game, for example, you can apply all of the hints given in this chapter to any WCW opponent. Finally, sports games are usually short and have limited scope. All of the action takes place in a single ring or field. Only the opponents vary from one challenge to the next.

Why am I telling you this? Is this Game Philosophy 101? Nope. The point is that you must approach sport games a little differently than you do arcade games. And the strategies that follow will reflect that difference. With that in mind, let's see how to become the WCW champ!

Strategies

Be careful when playing against the NES-controlled wrestler. As with most computerized sports games, the computer opponent performs almost flawlessly. Your foe will be quick to the punch or kick, so stay on your toes.

Learn the personalities of the wrestlers. Some are aggressive. Others walk right into your punches and kicks. For instance, Kevin Sullivan and Eddie Gilbert are a couple of tough cookies who attack relentlessly and are hard to keep down. Sting, on the other hand, is a wimp. But in any case, keep your guard up and do your best. Use the wimpy wrestlers to perfect your moves for later, more difficult matches.

Think Defensively

Avoid getting trapped between the ropes and your opponent. This predicament is almost impossible to escape without suffering severe damage.

Stay out of your foe's reach. As you become a Nintendo Master Wrestler, you'll learn how close you can get to an adversary without getting hit. Keep this distance. When your opponent attacks and misses, he'll move into your "strike zone." Sock it to him!

Outside the Ring

Although a wrestling match takes place in a ring, a lot of action happens outside the ropes. When a wrestler is hurt, it's easy to toss him over the ropes and get in some illegal bashing. Keep in mind, however, that you have only 20 seconds to get back into the ring. As you'll see, this can be to your advantage.

Soften your foe inside the ring with strong offensive attacks, then throw him from the ring and finish him off. When the audience tosses a weapon into the ring, get to it first and immediately use it on your opponent. If you hold it too long, you'll get socked, or, worse, your foe will return to the ring unscathed. If your enemy gets the weapon first, run for the safety of the ring—weapons can be used only outside the ring.

After throwing a wrestler over the ropes, try the following winning strategies.

Avoid your opponent until the timer hits 13 or 14, then kick or punch him into submission. Next, swing him into the wall. That should knock him onto his back. Now re-enter the ring just in time to watch the referee count your opponent out and disqualify him.

The second technique is similar but requires a quicker hand. Weaken your foe. As the timer hits 16 or 17, move between your opponent and the skirt of the ring. Because you're blocking him, your foe can't re-enter the ring. You can. Maintain this position until the count of 19 (I know—easier said than done). Quick, jump back in the ring. Do it right, and your opponent gets disqualified.

Feeling tough? Then let's see you claim that WCW belt.

SUPER SECRETS

Super Secrets!

Secrets

Disclaimer: *Although all of the codes and secrets given below have been tested, due to possible changes by the manufacturers, we cannot predict that they will work on every cartridge. Moreover, some sequences are extremely difficult to enter accurately and may require several attempts.*

Action Fighter: Enter the code SPECIAL to begin your game powered-up.

Adventure Island: If you jump just before the "G" sign at the end of area 1, you'll uncover an egg containing the Hudson bee. Pick up the bee for unlimited continues. Just press the left arrow then Start when your game is over.

Afterburner: When you see the "Game Over" screen, press A, B, and Select at the same time. You found the sound-test mode!

Alien Syndrome: During a two-player game, if you come across a weapon that both players want, have both players touch the weapon at the same time.

Arkanoid: Secret level select! While viewing the title screen, press Start, A, and B at the same time, and press Select five times.

Athena: Squat on a small red-spotted mushroom in area 1, and you'll get a dragon helmet, a fire sword, and a lion shield. You must find the right mushroom, though.

Bad Dudes: Want to start a game with 63 men? You bet! Enter this sequence on control pad two—B, A, down, up, down, up. Now press Start on control pad one.

Bases Loaded: Start your battle for the pennant with a 34-win/7-loss record by using this password: GEEDFBH. Also, for a no-hit game against the computer, try this: Use a left-handed pitcher and keep him on the left side of the mound for each pitch. Hold the down arrow during the pitch. The batter won't swing! In the fifth inning, bring in a different lefty pitcher and follow the same procedure.

Blaster Master: When battling the bosses of levels two, four, six, or seven, use the grenade weapon. The instant the grenade hits the boss, press the Start button to pause the game. Even though the action stops, the grenade continues to do its work. In a minute or so, unpause the game. The boss is dead!

Bomberman: Jump to stage 50 with this code:

FECPIANNMJGGKGIDJABA

Bubble Bobble: To select any level of play, enter the password DDFFI. Then use buttons A and B to change the level number.

Commando: While on the title screen, use controller 2 to enter the sequence—left, left, left, B, B, A, A, A, A, right, and Start. You've now exposed all the hidden ladders.

Contra: To start with 30 men, quickly enter the sequence —up, up, down, down, left, right, left, right, B, A, and Start. You not only start with 30 men, but you'll get 30 men when you continue too!

Deadly Towers: When the game begins, immediately let yourself be killed. Get the password and change the first two letters to EF or FE. When you enter this password, you'll start with extra strong defensive powers.

Double Dragon II: In stage 4, when the helicopter door opens, press the Pause button and wait a few seconds. When you unpause the game, the door will close.

Duck Tales: If your money for the current stage ends up being a number with a 7 in the ten thousandths place,

Launchpad will take you to a fabulous area filled with diamonds.

Faxanadu: Jump to the end of the game with this code:

q8f?cn?,SwSYzGYLhqSthCEA

Gauntlet: Stuck on a stun tile? To get off with minimum damage, press Start to pause the game. When you resume, you'll be able to move.

Goal: Jump directly to the finals with this password:

FTXAREZC GOLGPIMB

Godzilla: Want to try the ultimate challenge? Enter this password, making sure you use zeros in place of o's: DESTR0Y ALL M0NSTERS. To see the opening and closing scenes of the game, use the password START T0 END.

Golgo 13: Here's a secret that'll let you start at any stage. During the game demo, when you see a close-up of Golgo 13's eyes, tap the Start button on controller 1, then hold the up arrow, A, and B on that controller. Now on controller 2, have someone hold the up arrow, left, A, and B. While holding the buttons, press Start on controller 1. The number "00" will appear. Adjust this number using the up and down arrows on controller 1.

Gradius: Want a super-powered Warp Rattler? As soon as the game starts, pause it, then enter this sequence on the control pad: up, up, down, down, left, right, left, right, B, and A. Now unpause the game. To continue a game where you left off, wait for the "Game Over" display, then quickly punch in down, up, B, A, B, A, B, A, B, A.

Guardian Legend: Want to play only the space scenes and skip the labyrinths? Try this password: TGL. Jump to the last level with this password:

M7wTQVhUTRxWW3xUZlxy2x31!Dmj5fVh

Gun Smoke: Wait for the title screen, then press A, A, A, A, Select, Select, Select, Select, right, right, and Start. If you enter the code properly, you'll have a machine gun with 300 rounds.

Gyruss: In the Chance Stages, you can collect 30,000 bonus points by hitting the same number of ships as the number of the stage. For example, in stage 3, hit three ships to get the bonus. Also, at the title screen, press A, B, right, left, right, left, down, down, up, and up, and you'll get 30 free ships.

Ikari Warriors: Here's a secret code for continuing your game. When you lose your last life, enter the sequence A, B, B, A with the control pad buttons. Make sure you press the buttons before the "Game Over" screen appears.

Ikari Warriors II: See the hint above for Ikari Warriors. It works for the sequel too.

Jackal: In a two-player game, right when your partner is losing his last life, try pressing buttons A and B on your controller at the same time. If your timing is perfect, he may get hundreds of extra lives.

John Elway's Quarterback: When you get the ball, select normal or reverse play and wait for the time to run out. Now quickly pass to a teammate. He'll be able to run for a touchdown with no interference.

Karnov: To select a particular level, plug in both controllers, then hold down A, B, and Select and press the right arrow on controller 1. Press A on controller 2 to select the level.

Kid Icarus: To make yourself invincible and begin the game at the Overworld Fortress, use this code:

    ICARUS FIGHTS MEDUSA ANGELS.

To continue your game in the same position in which it ended, press B, A, and B on control 1 before the title is displayed.

Kid Niki: In level 3, get on the third rising and falling cloud. Then kill the kite and the bird, and ride the cloud all the way up. Press up arrow while jumping, and you'll find a secret room.

Kung-Fu Heroes: Hold down button A and press Start to continue a game where you were last killed.

Legacy of the Wizard: Use this code to begin your game with all available tools and weapons:

    C4TB RSSH 6RXC 1TJH CUTK 3NFT YWMC WJVU

Legend of Kage: If you kill seven ninjas with your sword while standing in a moat, a blue creature will appear. Catch him and you get a 1-up.

Life Force: Get 30 ships and four continues by entering this sequence during the title screen: up, up, down, down, left, right, left, right, B, A, and Start.

Metroid: Here's a strange one. Enter the password JUSTIN BAILEY, and Samus gets transformed into a woman. You'll also start with a bunch of weapons.

Monster Party: Jump to level 8 by entering the password:

DTvgs.iNT

Ninja Gaiden: If you want to hear the game's collection of sounds, wait till you see "Tecmo Presents 1989." Then hold down the left controller arrow, while simultaneously holding down Select, Start, A, and B. Now select sounds with up and down, and use A and B to start and stop sounds.

Phantom Fighter: Jump all the way to town 8 with this code:

7LXZ 7Y76 6H6D

P.O.W.: After the title screen appears, enter this sequence on your control pad: A, B, B, up, up, down, left, and Start. Twenty free men!

Racket Attack: Go right to any match from two to seven with the following six passwords:

JSLPVYC   GKVYLWC   PSFRCHC
KYIMYDD   IXKOWCD   RYTONMD

Rambo: To make your hero invincible, enter this password:

H800 lbW2 kG4Q KwKc 66WH QbW2 0F1D G19D

Renegade: Start at any mission, from two to four respectively, by entering these sequences:

Level 2	Hold the down arrow on control 2, and then press down, up, right, up, left, up, and Start on control 1.
Level 3	Hold the down arrow on control 2, and then press up, down, left, down, right, down, and Start on control 1.
Level 4	Hold the up arrow on control 2, and then press down, down, up, up, right, left, and Start on control 1.

Ring King: To get unlimited stamina, try this sequence requiring two controllers: Press A on controller 2. Press A, Select, and A on controller 1. Now press B on controller 2, and then Select on controller 1. Finally, on controller 2 press A and B at the same time, and then on controller 1, press B twice. Whew!

Robocop: After you use your last continue, when "Game Over" appears, hold down A, B, Select, and Start at the same time. Unlimited continues!

Spy Hunter: At the title screen, hold down Select, A, B, and the center of the arrow pad. When you press Start, your car will be packed with great weapons. To get ten free cars, at the beginning of a game, press the right arrow, Select, and Start at the same time.

Super Pitfall: To continue a game where you left off, at the title screen press Select, A, A, A, Select, and Start.

Tetris (Tengen version): To select any level up to 17, pause the game with the Start button, and then enter this sequence on the control pad: up, down, up, down, left, right, B, B, and A. Also, to convert any piece into a long red bar, pause the game and enter this sequence: up, up, down, down, left, right, left, right, B, and A. Though this always works the first time you try it, after that it's pot luck.

Tiger-Heli: When you lose your last man, hold down A and B before the title screen appears. You'll begin on the level on which you died.

Track & Field II: Here's a great way to claim the hammer throw world record. Keep your power meter as low as possible. Then when your on-screen character flashes, press A and throw the hammer at an 80 degree angle. The hammer won't go far, of course, but your mixed-up NES will record the throw as 92.04 meters. This is a tough one to do.

Trojan: To continue a game, press up arrow when the title screen appears, then press Start.

Who Framed Roger Rabbit?: Get a bunch of wallets! First go to Eddy's office and get the wallet in the wastebasket. Now leave the building, and get the wallet on the sidewalk. Re-enter the building and search the wastebasket for another wallet.

Repeat this sequence as often as you like, getting up to nine wallets. Also, stock up with this special code:

LLHHHHHH-ODHHOH-HHHHHHGZ.

Nothing will happen when you enter the code, but when you start the game, you'll be loaded!

Xevious: You know the lake right before the first set of spinning walls? Bomb the lake, and an "S" flag will pop up. Grab the flag for an extra ship.

Zanac: Want to jump immediately to any of the first ten levels? Press the Reset button on your NES 13 times, then press Select on the controller. Change the level number with the arrow pad, then press Start to play your selected level.

1943: To get an extra strong shot, press and hold the B button until you hear a tone.

8 Eyes: Here are passwords for the first, second, and third endings, respectively:

ONAPPMBPPF   CKBPPAAPEE   GBCPHAAHAD

This game also contains two secret expert levels of play. Access those levels with these passwords:

TAXANTAXAN   FINALSTAGE

MANUFACTURERS

Manufacturers

Acclaim Entertainment
71 Audrey Avenue
Oyster Bay, NY 11771
(516) 922-2400
Game counseling: (516) 624-9300

Capcom
3303 Scott Boulevard
Santa Clara, CA 95054
(408) 727-0400
Game counseling: (800) 843-4632

FCI
150 East 52nd Street
34th Floor
New York, NY 10022
(212) 753-8100
Game counseling: (312) 968-0425

Konami Inc.
815 Mittel Drive
Wood Dale, IL 60191
(312) 595-1443
Game counseling: (312) 350-1268

Nintendo of America Inc.
4820 150th Ave. NE
Redmond, WA 98052
(206) 882-2040
Game counseling: (206) 885-7529

Sunsoft
925 A.E.C. Drive
Wood Dale, IL 60191
(312) 350-8800
Game counseling: Same as above

Ultra Software Corp.
240 Gerry Street
Wood Dale, IL 60191
(312) 595-2874
Game counseling: (312) 350-1268